BY LISA MILLER

*The Spiritual Child: The New Science on Parenting
for Health and Lifelong Thriving*

*The Awakened Brain: The New Science of Spirituality
and Our Quest for an Inspired Life*

THE
AWAKENED
BRAIN

THE
AWAKENED
BRAIN

THE NEW SCIENCE OF SPIRITUALITY AND
OUR QUEST FOR AN INSPIRED LIFE

LISA MILLER, PhD

with Esmé Schwall Weigand

RANDOM HOUSE
NEW YORK

Published in the United States by Random House, an imprint and
division of Penguin Random House LLC, New York.

RANDOM HOUSE and the HOUSE colophon are registered trademarks
of Penguin Random House LLC.

Library of Congress Cataloging-in-Publication Data
Names: Miller, Lisa (Clinical psychologist), author.
Title: The awakened brain : the new science of spirituality
and our quest for an inspired life / Lisa Miller, PhD.
Description: New York : Random House, 2021.
Identifiers: LCCN 2020047036 (print) | LCCN 2020047037 (ebook) |
ISBN 9781984855626 (hardcover) | ISBN 9781984855633 (ebook)
Subjects: LCSH: Awareness. | Self-actualization
(Psychology) | Spirituality.
Classification: LCC BF311.M5165 2021 (print) |
LCC BF311 (ebook) | DDC 153—dc23
LC record available at https://lccn.loc.gov/2020047036
LC ebook record available at https://lccn.loc.gov/2020047037

PRINTED IN CANADA ON ACID-FREE PAPER

randomhousebooks.com

2 4 6 8 9 7 5 3 1

First Edition

Art by iStock/Ihor Reshetniak

To Phil, with love

Never cease to stand like curious children before the Great Mystery into which we were born.

—*Albert Einstein*

CONTENTS

AUTHOR'S NOTES

This book is intended to provide helpful information on the subjects discussed. It is not meant to be used to diagnose or treat any specific medical condition. Please be certain to consult with your own healthcare provider before making any decisions that affect your health.

Names and identifying details of some of the people portrayed in this book have been changed.

THE
AWAKENED
BRAIN

INTRODUCTION

ANYTHING TRUE CAN BE SHOWN

It was the summer of 2012. I hurried down the narrow, fluorescent-lit hallway of the psychiatry lab at Columbia University Medical School, coffee balanced in one hand, mind racing. Today our MRI (magnetic resonance imaging) team would finally get our eyes on the results of months and months of research. Ravi, the statistical analyst, caught up to me in the hall, his eyes wide, a stunned expression on his usually composed face. He held a stack of papers in his trembling hands.

"I ran the data many times," he said. "It's all very surprising."

For close to a year our team had been working long, hard hours to design and implement a cutting-edge study to peer into the brain to learn more about preventing depression. Ravi worked closest to the machines and statistics, steadily punching buttons, collecting data, modeling the findings, running numbers. Today he would show us a first glimpse of the results that would tell us whether or not spirituality plays a role in preventing or protecting against depression. I love every part of science— the push and beckon of a question, the challenge and rigor of finding the best way to test what is true—but I especially love *this* part of science: the first reckoning with the data. This would be our first thrilling view of where the numbers led and we hoped what we saw might help us toward a new possibility for alleviating mental suffering.

We live in an age of unprecedented mental anguish. Depression, anxiety, and substance abuse have reached epidemic proportions globally. In 2017, 66.6 million Americans—more than half of the respondents on the National Survey on Drug Use and Health—reported binge drinking within the past month, and 20 million met the criteria for a substance use disorder. Thirty-one percent of American adults will develop a full-blown anxiety disorder at some point in their lives, and 19 percent in any given year. The World Health Organization reports that 264 million people on the planet are depressed; depression is the third most costly disability worldwide. Each year, 17 million American adults are depressed. Over 16 percent of youth in late adolescence currently face depression, and the impact of depression on suicide accounts for *the second leading cause of death* in adolescents, rivaled only by death by auto accident.

At Columbia University, where I teach, eight students died by suicide in 2016–2017. A study of more than 67,000 college students across 108 institutions in the United States published in 2019 found that *20 percent* reported that they had engaged in self-harm such as cutting, *24 percent* reported suicidal ideation, and *9 percent* had attempted suicide.

While the stakes of our mental health crisis are truly life and death, many of us also suffer from less debilitating, though still painful, conditions: burnout and chronic stress; trouble concentrating and connecting; loneliness and isolation; lives that are rich in many ways yet feel somehow narrow, hollow, and cut off. Even when we experience success and satisfaction, we may sense that there's more to happiness—that life could be more joyful, rewarding, and meaningful.

It seems that every person I meet has a parent, child, sibling, partner, or close friend afflicted by depression, anxiety, substance abuse, or chronic stress. And there's not a lot on offer for those of us worried about a loved one, or struggling ourselves. Our mainstay treatments for depression—psychotherapy and anti-depressant medications such as SSRIs—provide some help to people, but for others have disappointing results. Only *half* of treated patients see a disappearance of symptoms within a year of intervention, while another 20 percent find only a partial reduction of symptoms; and the positive effects that are gained through medication are not enduring—when we stop taking the drugs, depression or anxiety often returns.

I hoped that today's lab meeting might reveal even an inkling of a sustainable solution to our devastating crisis in wellness and mental health. Ravi followed me into a crowded room and we squeezed into the last two open seats around the long wood laminate table. His fingers drummed the stack of papers.

He usually worked with a detached, skeptical cool. "We can run the data from the scanner," he'd said, "but I seriously doubt we'll find anything." Myrna, the MRI team's most senior colleague and the one who had secured the funding for this study, had agreed, saying, "I'd be *very* surprised if we find any kind of association between spirituality and depression, but we shall see."

Contemporary psychotherapy tended to characterize spirituality and religion as a crutch or defense, a set of comforting beliefs to lean on in hard times. In our field, spirituality was a barely studied, nearly invisible variable. Over the past twenty years of my career, I'd seen surprising clinical and epidemiological evidence that spirituality could have a protective benefit for our mental health. But could we discern a concrete physiological function of spirituality in our health and development? Was spirituality thus far invisible in the brain because it was insignificant to mental health or impossible to measure—or was it invisible because no one had yet looked?

Myrna cleared her throat and started the meeting.

"Let's take a few moments to review the initial MRI findings," she said. "I believe Ravi's compiled a handout with the new results."

Our team had used Myrna's multigenerational sample of clinically depressed and non-depressed women, and their children and grandchildren. We'd taken MRI scans of people at high and low genetic risk for depression to see if there were any patterns among the brain structures of depressed and non-depressed participants that could allow us to develop more targeted and effective treatments.

And we'd added a new—and controversial—question to our study. We'd asked all participants to respond to a major question used in the clinical science literature to quantify inner life: *How personally important is religion or spirituality to you?* In addition to comparing the brain structures of depressed and non-depressed candidates, we wanted to see how spirituality was associated with brain structure, and how spirituality correlated with risk for depression.

Ravi's face still looked stunned and his hands jittery as he passed his stack of papers around the room. I took a two-page color handout from the pile. It was still warm from the printer. My eyes raced over the page, taking in the results, looking for whatever it was that seemed to have rattled Ravi. It took only a moment for me to see it.

On the top half of the page was a black rectangle with two brain images inside. The scan on the left showed the composite brain image of participants with low spirituality—those who had reported that religion or spirituality was of medium, mild, or low importance. The scan on the right showed the composite brain of participants with sustained, high spirituality—those who had said religion or spirituality was of high personal importance.

The difference between the two images made my heart race and my spine tingle.

The brain on the left—the low-spiritual brain—was flecked intermittently with tiny red patches. But the brain on the right—the brain showing the neural structure of people with stable and high spirituality—had huge swaths of red, at least five times the size of the small flecks in the other scan. The finding was so clear and stunning, it stopped my breath.

The high-spiritual brain was healthier and more robust than the low-spiritual brain. And the high-spiritual brain was thicker and stronger in *exactly the same regions* that weaken and wither in depressed brains.

The room was utterly silent.

"It's not at all what we expected to see," Ravi said.

The air conditioner clanked on, a loud roar amid the stillness. Then a low chuckle rose from the back of the room.

"Well, well, Lisa," someone said.

My closest, most treasured colleagues had been skeptical. But the data was persuasive. Spirituality appeared to protect against mental suffering.

THE MRI FINDINGS marked a pivotal moment on the way to my breakthrough discovery that each of us has an **awakened brain**. Each of us is endowed with a natural capacity to perceive a greater reality and consciously connect to the life force that moves in, through, and around us. Whether or not we participate in a spiritual practice or adhere to a faith tradition, whether or not we identify as religious or spiritual, our brain has a natural inclination toward and docking station for spiritual awareness. The awakened brain is the neural circuitry that allows us to see the world more fully and thus enhance our individual, societal, and global well-being.

When we awaken, we feel more fulfilled and at home in the world, and we build relationships and make decisions from a wider view. We move from loneliness and isolation to connection; from competition and division to compassion and altruism; from an entrenched focus on our wounds, problems, and losses to a fascination with the journey of life. We begin to live beyond a "pieces and parts" model of identity and a splintered, fragmented view of who we are to one another, and to cultivate a way of being built on a core awareness of love, interconnection, and the guidance and surprise of life.

I didn't set out to study spirituality per se. My discovery of the awakened brain began with a desire to understand human resilience and help people who were struggling. Bit by bit, striking data points and my patients' stories of hurt and healing helped me see that spiritual experience was a vital, though overlooked, component of healing.

So what is spirituality? Many of us have had experiences we might describe as spiritual. A moment of deep connection with another being or in nature. A feeling of awe or transcendence. An experience of startling synchronicity or a time when a stranger showed up and did something that changed your life. A time you felt held or inspired or buoyed up by something greater than yourself—a higher power perhaps, but also nature or the universe or even the surge of connection at a concert or sporting event.

I'm a scientist, not a theologian. Faith traditions have a lot to say about ontological questions—the nature of reality, why we're here, the existence and guidance of God or a higher power. As a scientist, I don't address these issues. I look at how humans are built and how we develop over the life span.

I've discovered that the awakened brain is both inherent to our physiology and invaluable to our health and functioning. The awakened brain includes a set of innate perceptual capacities that exist in every person through which we experience love and connection, unity, and a sense of guidance from and dialogue with life. And when we engage these perceptual capacities—when we make full use of how we're built—our brains become structurally healthier and better connected, and we access unsurpassed psychological benefits: less depression, anxiety, and substance abuse; and more positive psychological traits such as grit, resilience, optimism, tenacity, and creativity.

The awakened brain offers more than a model for psychological health. It gives us a new paradigm for being, leading, and relating that can help us act with greater clarity and capability as we face humanity's greatest challenges. We can evolve our work and school culture toward greater purpose and meaning. We can revise our governments and health and social service institutions to better support and serve all. We can see our choices and the consequences of our actions through a lens of interconnectedness and shared responsibility. And we can learn to tap into a larger field of awareness that puts us in better touch with our inner resources, with one another, and with the fabric of all life.

An awakened brain is available to all of us, right here in our neural circuitry. But we have to choose to engage it. It's a muscle we can learn to strengthen, or let atrophy. I've come to see the problems we have in leadership, education, social justice, the environment, and mental health as different emanations of the same problem: *un*awakened awareness. A universal, healing capacity that has not been engaged or cultivated, that's been left to die on the vine. The problem is within. And so is the solution.

Each one of us has the ability to fully develop our innate capacity to live through an awareness of love, interconnection, and appreciation of life's unfolding. Beyond belief, beyond a cognitive story we tell ourselves, the awakened brain is the inner lens through which we access the truest and most expansive reality: that all of life is sacred, that we never walk alone. Our brains are wired to perceive and receive that which uplifts, illuminates, and heals.

My decades-long clinical, epidemiological, neuroscientific, and personal journey has led me through diverse terrain: from an inpatient psychiatric ward where a troubled patient made an unconventional request, to middle-aged suburban parents grappling with infidelity and divorce; from rural teenagers caught in the juvenile criminal system, to the highest leaders and decision makers at the Pentagon; from broad statistical research, to up-close, real-time brain imaging studies and examinations of our DNA; from growth and healing in my patients' and students' lives, to a startling transformation in my own.

This book is the story of how I discovered the awakened brain, why it matters, and how we can cultivate it in daily life.

And it's the story of human possibility—of all the ways we're cut down and cut off in life, and how we become whole.

CHAPTER 1

NOTHING COULD HAVE BEEN DONE

A long, low howl broke the early morning quiet of the ward, followed by a scream. I rushed out of the cramped office where interns and residents filled out charts, ready to assist whoever was in distress. Before I could locate the source of the scream, a nurse hurried around the corner balancing a tray of bottles and sterile syringes and disappeared into a patient's room. Soon all was quiet again. Fluorescent lights glared off the manila-colored walls and gray linoleum floors.

It was the fall of 1994. I'd recently finished my doctoral program at the University of Pennsylvania and had chosen a clinical internship as a psychologist at a psychiatric inpatient unit in Manhattan, part of a network of premier university hospitals at the epicenter of clinical advances in psychotherapy and mental health. Because the clinical approach and standard of care would have been similar at any other major American urban hospital, I'll call the ward Unit 6. (All names and identifying details of the patients have been changed.) The patients on Unit 6 were diverse in ethnicity and age, many poor, many with rough lives and recurrent diagnoses, many also grappling with substance abuse. Sometimes they were brought to the hospital emergency room by the police against their will, to prevent suicide or homicide.

This wasn't a top-choice hospital—patients with good insurance often went elsewhere—but it wasn't a final stop, either. To come here wasn't the equivalent of being "sent upstate," the euphemism many medical staff and patients used to refer to a long-term mental illness facility in northern New York. Yet all of the patients I'd met here had been admitted and readmitted numerous times, their files three or four inches thick. I was one of four interns on the ward, each of us serving two residents at a time, as well as a caseload of eight through our outpatient clinic. We started each day with a team meeting at eight o'clock sharp, the staff of psychiatrists, psychologists, social workers, nurses, and aides gathering around a table to hear updates from the night before—what the patients had eaten, how they'd groomed and slept, if there'd been any behavioral episodes. "Mr. Jones was malodorous," an aide would report. "Ms. Margaret refused dinner." Basic health and grooming habits can be tied to aspects of mental health—yet it always struck me as odd that on a ward dedicated to the healing of inner struggle we spent so much time talking about the physical body. Most patients wore hospital gowns, not street clothes, as though they were at the hospital for surgery or for treatment of a physical illness that required them to stay in bed.

I'd noticed the same phenomenon the first time I set foot on a psychiatric ward in the mid-1970s, when I was about eight years old. My beloved Grandma Eleanor, who had commuted back and forth from Iowa all the way to the University of Chicago to study psychology, took me to visit her dear friend who'd been hospitalized, someone she'd grown up with and stayed close to over the decades. The friend was not actually related to me, but I'd always known her as Aunt Celia. In the hospital, I was confused to discover that she didn't appear to be sick. She wasn't wearing any bandages that I could see. She wasn't hooked up to any machines. She had a radiant smile, a knowing sense of humor. And yet, like the other patients on her floor, with pain visible in their faces, or eyes gone distant, she was confined to a narrow bed in a small room. I was struck by the suffering I sensed in many patients there, and by how isolated Aunt Celia and the others appeared. Later, I would learn that Grandma Eleanor was known for a legacy of activism, working constructively with state hospitals to bring psychotherapy to patients in institutions where they were only being injected, or put in straitjackets, or given shock therapy, and that she advocated for patients like Aunt Celia to be moved to eldercare homes where they could receive ongoing medical attention while also enjoying a greater sense of community and support.

In many ways, mental health treatment standards had considerably improved in the twenty years since I'd visited Aunt Celia. The thirty-five patients on Unit 6 weren't restrained in straitjackets, or locked up and forgotten. We operated as a therapeutic community, patients participating in large and small psychotherapy groups each week, as well as short daily check-ins with their assigned doctor. The residents could move freely on the ward and engage in conversation or activities in the community room. The staff had top-notch training and cared deeply about the patients.

Our psychological treatment model was primarily psychodynamic. We'd been trained to help patients comb the past for insights and awareness that could release their present suffering. If patients could understand their anger or childhood wounds, the theory went, they could release them and no longer be controlled by them. The way out of suffering was to face suffering and gain insight. To excavate painful memories and experience discomfort in order to advance awareness.

On the psychiatric side, the ward took a psychopharmacological approach, using medications to ameliorate or eradicate symptoms. I was grateful for the medications that provided relief to patients in acute pain. Yet in my first weeks on the ward I began to wonder if we could do more to support patients' long-term healing, to interrupt the constantly revolving door between in- and outpatient services.

After the morning team meeting, the interns would go see our individual patients, stopping by their rooms or finding them on the unit to see how they were doing. I wondered what it was like for patients in their forties, fifties, sixties, and older, who'd suffered for decades, who were on their sixth or seventh admission to the ward, to have a twenty-six-year-old intern who'd been practicing for all of three weeks show up unannounced for a twenty-minute conversation, the young intern in professional clothes, the seasoned patient in a flimsy, open-backed gown, knowing the whole process would begin again in six months when the current batch of interns left to begin their next rotation. Did we really know more about the nature of our patients' suffering than they did themselves? Might there be a different path? A way to analyze and pathologize less, and hear more?

As summer bent toward fall, the more frustrated I became with an approach that seemed unhelpful at best, and, at worst, a tragic dead-end. We could offer a temporary, medication-induced reprieve from painful symptoms, or a slightly better understanding of why a childhood trauma had been so derailing. Neither outcome promised real healing. And when a patient opened up with an authentic expression that didn't quite fit our psychoanalytic mold, we sometimes shut the door.

I co-led a weekly group with a fellow intern who had a strong, verging on inflexible, theoretical view. He thought the purpose of group psychoanalysis was to interpret and release our projections. He wanted patients to interpret what they made of one another and see how they misunderstood one another as projections of their injured psyches. One week a woman who was diagnosed with schizophrenia stepped outside the choreography. "I love to pray," she said, "but when I'm having symptoms and I try to pray, I don't hear my prayers the same way." I turned toward her. "Wow," I said, leaning in, inviting her to say more. But the other intern cut her off. She tried to speak again and he waved his hand impatiently, dismissively. The room grew quiet. "So you see me as what?" he said. "A bully? Do you see me taking control?" Somehow the patient was supposed to figure out he wanted her to interpret how she saw him as a projection of a feeling or experience from long ago. To this day I regret that I didn't push back and hold space for the patient. That I didn't turn to her and say, "What were you saying about your prayer life?" I decided I would never let the door be closed on patients again. That if they opened a door, I would hold it open.

It sometimes seemed that instead of helping patients get better, we were making them worse. Reinforcing a burden. Handing them a deterministic perspective. Teaching them that the sum of their lives would never amount to more than the effects of whatever terrible, inescapable thing might have happened in the past. That the best they could hope to achieve was a clearer understanding of how they'd suffered, and of how their suffering had written the rest of their lives. The bulk of our patients returned to the ward multiple times over the course of decades, one psychoanalytic therapist after another helping them construct a more and more entrenched narrative of how they had been broken by what had happened when they were young.

One of my first patients on the ward was Mr. Danner, a man in his mid-fifties with a wardrobe of bell-bottoms and leather jackets and feathered hats straight out of the 1970s Harlem nightclub scene where he'd dealt and become addicted to heroin as a young man. Almost all of his friends from that time were dead. He was still using, his legs, arms, and neck riddled up and down with pockmarks from shooting up. He'd been admitted to the ward so many times for aggressive behavior and delusional psychotic outbursts over the last twenty years that his file included two folders, each one five inches thick.

He was fifty-six, but he looked eighty-six, his body hollowed out and hunched, his jutting shoulder blades sharp and pinched through his shirt. He walked with a cane, one of his legs almost too stiff to move. His uneven hair, shadowed face, and unwashed clothes reinforced the impression of his deterioration, but in his square jaw and expressive light brown eyes I could also see a glimpse of the man he'd been, his good looks and swagger.

At our first session he cut straight to his childhood trauma. "It was a cold winter in North Carolina," he began. "I was four years old and I was staring into my mother's coffin."

I was moved by his story of wrenching loss, of being shuttled from relative to relative after his mother's death, landing in New York as a young teen, chasing after parties and drugs as though still trying to warm the chill of that indelible winter day.

When we met a second time, he started our conversation the same way. "I was four years old and I was staring into my mother's coffin." Again, on our third visit, the same story, sad and haunting as ever, but told in a way that seemed increasingly rote and dissociated, as though he were fulfilling an obligation. I looked back through the earliest entries in his file and discovered the same early childhood memory referenced on page after page of clinical notes. Through decades of treatment he'd kept reliving the same cold, bereft moment. And it seemed in some ways that his therapy on the ward had reinforced his living there. Round and round through the revolving door of his admissions and discharges and readmissions, he'd been asked the same questions by each new intern. How did he feel about that moment? What were his insights about that moment? He'd been trained to fixate on that memory, but when he talked about it, it didn't seem full of his current psychological energy.

I started asking him questions outside the psychoanalytic mold. "How are you doing *now*?" I'd ask. "What happened this week? What's new?" Questions that brought him back into the present. He'd adjust himself, sit up straighter, reposition the cane he held between his legs, and lean forward, looking me in the eye.

"I rode the subway one day, a few years ago, right next to a woman in a fur coat," he said on one visit. "We made small talk. She didn't know the whole time I was sitting there I had a gun under my coat, that I was off to do something bad."

A psychoanalyst is trained to meet this kind of remark as a challenge, to take back control, to say, "Are you trying to rile me?" But each time he told me about a bad thing he'd done— and he had done cruel things, committed armed robberies, slept with his wife without telling her he was HIV-positive—I got the sense that he was essentially asking, "Can I count on you? Is your caring real, or do you see me as unworthy?"

There can sometimes be an amoral quality to psychoanalysis. An emotional distance. The patient acknowledges feelings of rage or hate and the analyst might look on with a blank stare and nod. There's often nothing relational or life-affirming. The therapeutic model can help improve impulse control, but it doesn't always call forth or guide the patient's best, authentic self. I was young and inexperienced, especially on guard against doing anything unprofessional. But I sensed that healing couldn't happen at a distance, that personal care and connection had to be part of the equation. So I diverged from a strictly psychoanalytic program. I listened, I bore witness, I saw it as my primary role not to excavate Mr. Danner's wounds or push him to be accountable for his wrongs, but to hold him in deep respect and regard. Writing this now, I'd go even further; I'd say that I held him in love.

Bit by bit, I noticed changes. He started bathing regularly and he cut his hair. He said he planned to stay clean from drugs when he left the ward. And during his first weeks in outpatient care, he did manage to stay off heroin. One day he came into the clinic with a spring in his usually labored gait. "I want to tell you something," he said. For the first time in as long as he could remember, he'd cashed his disability check and walked into a restaurant. "I sat down. The waiter came and asked me what I wanted. I ordered a steak. The waiter came with my food. I took out my knife and fork. I ate my meal. I paid the bill." He sat up tall and gave me a big smile, his eyes beaming with satisfaction.

On the surface, it was such a simple act. He'd ordered a meal and paid for it. But he told me about the experience with such engagement and dignity. This wasn't a hollowed-out circling of an old trauma. This was a fresh experience that showed a renewed self-respect and involvement with life. He was still homeless and in struggle. *And* he saw himself as worthy of eating in a restaurant, of asking for what he wanted, of being served.

At the end of the appointment he stood up, head held high.

I'd later learn he stayed clean for his longest stretch of sobriety since he started using in his late teens or early twenties. The good run didn't last. He'd start using again and be readmitted to the ward eighteen months after I stopped treating him. Ten years later, I'd read in a police blotter that he'd been arrested for armed robbery. Even as an idealistic intern, I hadn't had any illusions about how hard his life was or how difficult it would be for him to recover from decades of addiction and the concomitant struggles of poverty and isolation, to name a few. But the positive clinical changes I'd witnessed were enough to validate that the relational bond plays a role in healing, that the psychoanalytic framework of projection, transference, countertransference, ego, and rage is an a priori concept that's useful to a point, but not always sensitive to the direction of growth and recovery.

I didn't know that in treating Mr. Danner I'd taken my first step toward defining a new model for treatment. But I was growing to understand that there were limitations in the care we offered, and I was looking and listening for other possibilities.

MEDICATIONS DISPENSED, the ward returned to quiet that September morning, and several patients shuffled into the hallway and began heading toward the community room where we held daily meetings, mandatory for all patients and their doctors. In almost three months on the ward, I'd learned it was best to walk with patients because often it was during these unstructured, transitional times when a typically withdrawn or quiet patient would choose to share something important. At the end of the hallway my new patient, Lewis Danielson, stood in the doorway to his room, door ajar.

Lewis was a slim man in his early forties, with dark hair and pale skin, his eyes often unfocused and his speech somewhat slurred from the medications prescribed to mute his pain. Today he seemed unusually alert and animated.

"Dr. Miller," he said, beckoning me. "Come here." This was the geography of the ward—the most important communication happened in back corners, in the tight triangles behind half-open doors.

"Dr. Miller," he said again, his voice urgent.

But just as I reached him, a nurse making her morning medication round arrived at his room and handed him a Dixie cup piled high with pills.

"I'll wait while you take them," she said.

Lewis gave me a quick, lucid glance, and then turned his eyes to the floor as he methodically swallowed the pills.

I walked with him to the morning meeting, hoping he might share whatever it was he'd wanted to tell me so urgently, but he kept his gaze on the floor and didn't say another word. Like many patients on the ward, Lewis was given medications to suppress hallucination and delusion. Most patients on Unit 6 had been diagnosed with schizoaffective disorder—like Lewis—or with bipolar or major depressive disorder. But diagnosing patients was often like throwing darts at the wall—equal parts guesswork and chance. In the absence of a clear or effective treatment plan, the residents were routinely medicated to dull their pain and to suppress their volatile and sometimes violent behavior. The unit chief, a short, dark-haired Italian American man in his early fifties, known on the ward for his genuine caring and kind smile, had once told me, "The fact that we have medication is an act of grace." He was right. The drugs did muffle patients' discomfort and prevent outbursts. But the medication also made them foggy and lethargic, sometimes unable to control their own muscle movements. They would often drool, or their limbs would jerk in involuntary spasms. I was beginning to wonder if our role was more to mute the patients' symptoms than to heal their inner suffering.

As Lewis and I joined the other patients and staff in the community room for the daily meeting, there was no warmth in the room, even with the autumn sunshine spilling in through the large windows. Though the purpose of the meetings was to build community and engage in group therapy, everything felt impersonal. There was no coziness to the shabby furnishings or minimal decor. Plastic chairs were arranged in a huge oval, the plastic wood-veneer tables pushed to the edges of the room. The air smelled sharply of cleaning agent and cafeteria food.

Lewis and the other patients sat slumped with their arms crossed and bodies rigid, staring at their feet, speaking only if forced to. Even before the meeting had begun, they appeared anxious, beholden, powerless, and paranoid. The meetings often felt more like sentencing hearings, with patients terrified that saying the wrong thing would commit them to the ward for another week. I wasn't sure if the staff was deliberately using anxiety to fuel insight, but it didn't seem to be helping patients heal.

I took my place in the oval of chairs and greeted several patients near me: Rebecca Rabinowitz, a woman in her late thirties, with dark hair and blue eyes, had been experiencing severe depressive episodes for more than fifteen years, and had been admitted to the ward most recently for attempted suicide by overdose; Bill Manning, in his early forties, had been nearly incapacitated by bipolar disorder since he was in college; Jerry Petrofsky, one of my individual psychotherapy patients, in his early sixties, a city engineer known in the community for bicycling around the West Side, was admitted for attempting suicide during a bout of acute depression in reaction to a leukemia diagnosis.

I looked around the room for Esther Klein, a woman in her early seventies who had always reminded me of the women I knew from the synagogue my husband, Phil, and I sometimes attended. She appeared robust and healthy—but I knew from staff meetings that she was a Holocaust survivor. Her doctor believed that in order to heal, she needed to face her suffering. He'd pushed her during group and individual therapy to revisit her worst memories again and again. She had reluctantly spoken a few times at morning meetings about how she had escaped the death camps by living in hiding. Once, she told about a time she'd been forced to lick up vomit from the floor. Despite her doctor's best intentions, requiring her to describe her worst memories didn't seem to help her. Recently, I'd noticed her facial expressions were becoming flatter and more distanced, her arms wrapped more tightly around her body. She had grown noticeably more anxious and removed, as though the terrible past was sucking her backward. Today I didn't see her anywhere in the circle.

The psychiatrist running the meeting leaned forward in his chair and cleared his throat, signaling that the meeting had begun.

"I'd like to introduce our guest, Mr. Lawrence, from the hospital's administrative office." He gestured toward a visitor I'd never met, an authoritative-looking man in a dark suit.

"Yes, good morning," Mr. Lawrence said. "I have an unfortunate item to address." He held up a thick patient file. "I regret to inform the community of the passing of one of our longtime patients, Esther Klein."

My stomach dropped.

A fellow intern leaned close and whispered in my ear, "She committed suicide last night. Can you believe it? Right before the High Holidays."

"Esther had a long and painful life," Mr. Lawrence continued. "I have read the patient's file. It's a sad story, but nothing could have been done."

Looking around the room at the dozens of patients, I sud-

denly saw them as victims of institutionalization rather than patients getting the care they needed: Lewis, whose earlier urgency
had vanished behind a fog of medication, and who now stared
vacantly at the wall. Rebecca, who spoke in apologetic tones,
often expressing guilt and inadequacy. Bill, known on the ward
for being highly volatile, attempting to bridge his alienation
through bullying and disruptive behavior—angry outbursts,
crude sexual overtures, wall pounding. Jerry, perpetually sullen,
rarely rising from bed. They might leave the ward for a time, and
then they would be back. What were we really offering them?

Mr. Lawrence closed the file on Esther's life, and the meeting
continued, but everyone in the room seemed tense—faces flat,
bodies rigid, hands gripping the plastic armrests of the chairs.
Esther was dead—one of us, someone who had sat within our
circle. The announcement had come from a stranger who had
dealt with the crisis in a sterile, minimal way, with no time or
space allowed to process what had happened or mourn the loss.
We were gathered for the purpose of therapy, and yet the tone
and process were the opposite of therapeutic. I knew that later
the staff would hold a post-morbidity meeting, but the purpose
was more to cover the hospital legally. We wouldn't be invited to
respond to Ms. Klein's death in a personal way, or to reflect on
our clinical techniques, on the fact that the only treatment she'd
been offered had forced her to relive her trauma until the anguish had become unbearable. We were supposed to carry on as
though a preventable death hadn't happened on our watch.

Just then my patient Jerry spoke into the silence. His face was
red, his voice clipped. "What's being done for Yom Kippur?" he
demanded.

Many of the patients and doctors, myself included, were Jewish. Yom Kippur, the Day of Atonement, is the holiest day in

Judaism, a time of forgiveness and renewal after Rosh Hashanah, the start of the Jewish New Year. Before you ask God for forgiveness, you ask forgiveness of those you have harmed, and then you're cleansed of your sins. Many of the staff would be away in observance of the holiday. But religion was spoken of so rarely on the ward that even though Jerry was my patient, I'd had no idea he was Jewish. And I hadn't considered the fact that no service would be available for the many Jewish patients.

The presiding psychiatrist said that nothing was planned.

Rebecca raised her eyes as though searching for someone, then dropped them. Bill beat his fists against his thighs.

"*Nothing* is planned?" Jerry fumed. "*Nothing?*"

THAT EVENING I waited for the subway—the living lab, as I called it. The platform was full of high school kids traveling in packs, yelling and joking; exhausted-looking elderly people carrying bags of groceries; a terribly thin man holding a sign: HIV POSITIVE, JUST OUT OF THE HOSPITAL, NEED MONEY FOR A MEAL, GOD BLESS. The air was muggy and smelled of old tires and damp basements. When the train screeched to a stop, I lurched on board, finding a spot between the moms and nannies jostling strollers into the car, pulling young kids onto their laps, and the well-groomed men in sumptuous suede and pinstripe jackets and silken ties reaching for newspapers as they found a place at the handrail, their expressions absorbed yet somehow vacant. I looked carefully at the faces all around me. Many people were visibly suffering. The woman with wild eyebrows and coarse gray hair dyed a brassy orange, dirty cheeks creased with wrinkles, ranting and muttering. The young woman with soft, milky dark skin who called quietly up the car, half-singing her plea: "Me and my baby daughter need a dollar to get to the shelter tonight." The man in a worn-looking full-length wool coat, his body still trembling with the effort it had required to sit down.

Other passengers showed no outward signs of distress. They appeared to have homes and money and good health, they carried briefcases or bags from department stores, tissue paper rustling out of the top. Their faces didn't cave in despair or trouble or strain. But they still had a walled-off look, their brows furrowed, their eyes cast deep into their newspapers or their laps. They looked so dissatisfied and burdened and checked-out. As if the weight of the world bore down on them, and something vital was missing.

The clinical term for this is "dysthymia"—the low-grade feeling that life is unfulfilling. It feels like emptiness. Hunger. Disillusionment. Life is not what you'd hoped. It's a less severe version of what I saw every day on the inpatient ward: alienation, isolation, futility, darkness.

And it's what I recognized in my husband and many of our friends. We were young, in our twenties, full of energy and professional drive, committed to living and working in a way that contributed to the world. But sometimes the rush and buzz of our day-to-day felt more like treadmill than calling. Phil especially hated the elevator ride to and from his corporate law office each day, the way people boarded, raised a hand in greeting, and then looked down at their feet. It was like living on the two-dimensional rendering of an office set. It looked adequate from far away, but up close the whole thing was fake—and terribly lonely. We talked incessantly with our friends about work promotions and apartment upgrades. Almost every sentence began, "If I can just make it through x, y, z . . . ," then I can advance, then I can rest, then I can be happy. Among successful friends who had the educations, opportunities, jobs, friends, and romantic partners they'd always wanted, it seemed from our conversations that there was still an emptiness. A near-constant craving. A sense that life was not as meaningful or joyful as it might have been. As though we were on a never-ending staircase toward fulfillment, happiness always just out of reach.

The suffering in the world seemed so pervasive and relentless. I resolved that at the very least I would try to do something to help Jerry and Bill and the other patients on Unit 6.

CHAPTER 2

THE EMPTY KITCHEN

What, so now you're going to be a rabbi?" Phil asked that night when I told him about Jerry's question.

We stood shoulder-to-shoulder in our sports-car-sized kitchen, spooning Chinese takeout onto mismatched plates. Small as our apartment was, it was a step up from the one we'd just left. Our old apartment was a one-bedroom unit on the first floor of a narrow building, with just one window that looked out on the dark alley between our building and the stained brick building next door. Manhattan was a far cry from the wide-open spaces of my youth—the oak-lined Iowa street where I'd been born and the manicured suburban neighborhood of St. Louis where I'd grown up. But I loved that apartment. It was my first home with Phil. We had recently moved into a brownstone walk-up on West 76th and Columbus, near the American Museum of Natural History and Central Park West, where I went running, the neighborhood teeming with florist shops and at least a dozen brunch spots where we regularly met up with friends.

We brought our steaming food to the table and I opened a window. Voices floated up from the street below, car horns, the rush of late commuters racing home before nightfall.

"It's an important holiday," I said. "I thought I could at least offer a space for people who want to do a service." The hospital was in one of the most concentrated Jewish neighborhoods in the world. It seemed a huge oversight not to offer services. Besides, though I wasn't a by-the-book Jew, I did love the prayers and rituals. Maybe an informal service could bring a small peace to the ward.

"Isn't hospitalization the best excuse *not* to go to services?" Phil teased, lifting an egg roll off his plate.

When he joked, I could see the person he'd been when we met in the summer of 1985. I was nineteen, on the first day of a college summer internship working on campaign finance reform in Washington, DC. I'd arrived early for orientation—so early that the office was still dark, the door locked. I was camped out on one of the chairs in the small foyer when the elevator dinged and Phil emerged. He was tall and lanky, with dark curly hair, and he wore a somber suit and a bright blue and kelly-green tie.

"It's you," he said.

Apparently, on his walk to the internship office that morning in the nearly empty Northwest DC neighborhood, he'd noticed a young woman walking down K Street a block or so ahead of him, her gait fierce, her blond ponytail bouncing up and down like a piston. Her route matched his exactly. Every time he made a turn, he'd see her up ahead again.

"You seemed to be focused on your destination," he said. "Now I can see why." He gave me a wry smile and gestured toward the locked office door.

Our romance blossomed quickly that summer, and seven years later we were still wildly in love, the only married couple among our set of twentysomething friends. But in other ways it seemed that we were on a downhill slope away from that initial brightness. Phil had been an English major at Duke, and a drug counselor for a while in Camden, New Jersey, during the height of the crack epidemic. The experience had inspired him to go to law school; he wanted to become a district attorney and help put Miami drug lords behind bars. But I cautioned him away from what I feared would be a dangerous life, and he'd gone straight from law school to his current job on the fifty-sixth floor of a downtown Manhattan high-rise. We had a safe and comfortable life—but amid the daily noise and minor stresses, trying to sustain a thought while joining the press of bodies on the subway or running for the elevator, I sometimes felt that we'd traded richness for hollowness, openness for narrowness. That in choosing to play it safe, we were cutting ourselves off from a fuller life. "I'll work another six months," Phil had recently told me. But in six months, would he really quit? Or would he decide to work another year so we could save for a baby or our next apartment that would be only slightly less tiny than the one we lived in?

I didn't yet have the science to explain it, but we were beginning to suffer from choices made through what I would later understand to be our achieving brains, chasing down sensible goals—of advancement, protection—that would not fulfill us, that would cultivate stress and fear and disconnection, because outward goals are no substitute for larger meaning and purpose. We were living half-awake, and I didn't yet know the importance of awakening—much less how to do it.

While Phil tidied up the kitchen after our meal, I dug around in the boxes where I stored my grad school psychology books. At last I found it: my grandmother's old prayer book. It had first belonged to her mother, my great-grandmother, who had brought it over on the boat from Russia. My grandmother had inscribed her name and address inside the front cover: *Harriet Aliber Friedman, 311 51st Street, Des Moines, Iowa.* Perhaps her fellow congregants at Temple B'nai Jeshurun sometimes went home with the wrong prayer book. Grandma made sure she held on to hers. It was the same book that my sweet, soulful mother had used when she studied for her bat mitzvah the year she turned fifty, somehow catalyzed by the second half of life to ever deepen her spirituality. The binding of the book was frayed, the pages soft from years of being turned. I held it carefully, half afraid it might fall apart in my hands.

A WEEK LATER, when I arrived for our Yom Kippur observance at the Unit 6 kitchen—a windowless, antiseptic room with a round plastic table sitting on a tired-looking beige-and-white linoleum floor—they were already there: four Jewish participants and their supportive attendants. Rebecca, Bill, and Jerry had come, and so had Sol Stein, a thirty-eight-year-old admitted to the ward for barricading himself in a midtown hotel room and then struggling with the police officers who eventually pulled him out. He had such a fear of others that social interactions could trigger psychosis. He managed his social phobia through extreme isolation; he rarely left his room on the unit.

They had arranged the chairs in a circle and were seated as if at their own kitchen table, inhabiting the depressing room with a sense of intimacy and warm solemnity. This was the first time I'd seen residents interacting this way. It was normal to see patients in the common room with their chairs pulled up to a wall, or the more volatile people picking fights. In contrast, Rebecca, Jerry, Bill, and Sol were visibly here to connect. They'd dressed up in slacks, sweaters, button-up shirts. Rebecca had put on dark pink lipstick.

Given how socially withdrawn the four were, especially Sol, I wasn't sure to what extent they would participate in the prayers. But when I began the service, all four immediately commenced chanting, building into a robust chorus. Jerry, though he'd never said a word to me about being Jewish, recited whole passages of Hebrew text from memory. Bill tapped his foot along to the prayers, and Rebecca, usually so remote and guarded, leaned forward, her posture open. We conversed about the service as we went, everyone collaborative and gracious, taking turns reading sections in English, interpreting the holiday prayers, sharing insights. The attendants, usually called on to restrain patients or enforce rules, also seemed absorbed in the fluid rhythm of the prayers; though they were unfamiliar with the service, their presence and sensitivity added reverence.

We made our way through the service as I recalled it from my childhood. I was no scholar or expert, so I relied on what my mother had explained was the purpose of Yom Kippur—to acknowledge our sins and request forgiveness, to express gratitude for our lives, to confirm our identity as Jews. The patients became dramatically enlivened as the service progressed, their eyes brightening as we read and sang. Rebecca sat up taller and sang fully, without her usual muted tone. Jerry read robustly. Sol started to officiate and correct us on the mechanics of the service. When we reached a rough patch with the Hebrew, he led us through the pronunciation. Bill, despite being filled with energy, did not erupt in a manic display. He rocked assuredly with his eyes closed as he sang. The attendants, though they weren't Jewish, sang too, all of us joined together in an unlikely universal congregation.

Near the end, we paused the formal service to each offer a word about our individual experience of Yom Kippur. Jerry offered, "How can you not believe in an all-powerful God of goodness when you look around and see the beauty of the universe!"

I was completely stunned to hear such a confident statement of faith from my patient who usually lay in bed, trapped in a state of despair and futility.

Rebecca was next. "Thank you for the service, I have nothing to say."

My turn came. "Yom Kippur for me is very important because I make mistakes," I said. "I mess up. This is a time when I ask the people in my life forgiveness and then ultimately ask God for forgiveness."

Sol turned to me. "God will forgive you," he said. "God always forgives everyone."

Again, I was stunned. Sol, who feared people to the point of barricading himself in a hotel room, was offering me counsel, extending himself to care for me.

When it was Bill's turn, he bashfully confessed, "I'd like to apologize to God for cheating on my diabetic diet . . . but God knew all along." We all laughed.

The room felt cleansed and fresh, those of us around the table more connected to one another, and to something much bigger. But I had no reason to believe that the changed attitudes or atmosphere would carry back to normal life on the ward.

LATER THAT DAY I was in the interns' office, doing paperwork, when someone knocked on the door. Sol stood on the threshold, shoulders squared. He reached out his hand. "I want to thank you again for the service," he said. And then he emphasized what he had told me earlier: "God will forgive you. He always forgives."

That evening, after I'd packed up for the day and was heading down the hall to leave, Rebecca rushed up behind me. "I had a realization during the service," she said. "I always knew that Yom Kippur meant you could do penance for your sins. I knew you could admit to being wrong. But the service showed me that I could be forgiven. I had never realized this before." In her long years of severe depression, Rebecca had relegated her entire existence to an apology. She seemed guilty to exist at all. But now she was communicating something completely antithetical to her core view of herself.

For Sol and Rebecca and the other patients, the service had loosened the hold of a prison. It wasn't just that they appeared uplifted by the ceremony—it was that each person was more connected and restored in exactly the place where they were habitually cut off or occluded. The ceremony seemed, with laser precision, to have brought light into each person's darkest corner. Rebecca expressed feelings of self-worth; Sol exhibited deep connection and caring for others; Bill seemed steadier and more integrated; and Jerry articulated gratitude and appreciation for life. I had no idea why or how, no reason to trust that it would last. But something had happened in the back kitchen that wasn't happening through the primary medical interventions of medication and psychotherapy—and the healing, however temporary it might turn out to be, was specific to each patient's greatest need.

As a clinician—and as a scientist—I wanted to know: What had really happened at our Yom Kippur? Were patients uplifted by the familiar sense memories, by feeling at home culturally, practicing rituals they'd grown up with? Or was it the dignity of coming together, not as people with pathologies and treatment files but as fellow observers, that had brightened them, meeting in the back kitchen the way we might have met a different year at the neighborhood synagogue? Did the blast of illumination each patient had received offer anything of substance to practitioners working to support their longer-term healing?

Before leaving that day, I raised the question with my clinical supervisor. She listened thoughtfully. Finally, she said, "Lisa, it was very nice that you came in on your own religious holiday, and I can hear that the service was comforting to the patients. But the bottom line for them is a lifetime of medical illness. These patients are very sick. And that's our bottom line, too. This is a hospital."

Her implication was clear: spirituality was off-limits in our profession. I'd broken an unspoken rule—and I'd discredited myself by buying into a belief system that wasn't in keeping with medicine's rigor.

The conversation was over.

I WENT FOR a run that evening, heading north on Central Park West to the natural history museum, where I crossed into the park, following paths that wound through North and East Meadows, around the pond, through the woodsy Ramble, and down to Bethesda Fountain. I'd been a distance runner since high school when my father, a theater professor at Washington University in St. Louis, had received a major promotion, and our family moved east so he could accept his new post in the performing arts school at Boston University. Because I wanted to log as many miles as possible, I joined the boys' cross-country team, ran road races, and was an unofficial contestant in the Boston Marathon when I was fifteen, back when it was considered okay to spontaneously jump in and run the race. I'd been interviewed at the starting line in Hopkinton, apparently the young-est female at that time to have attempted the race. At the finish line down in Boston, two girls from my new high school, girls I'd met only a few times, embraced me like lifelong friends, eyes full of tears. Nobody in my family had envisioned that I would make it 26.2 miles to the finish, so they weren't there to greet me. A kind manager from a local Wendy's invited me in and of-fered me anything I wanted to eat to celebrate. The next week my mother took me to the doctor, worried about the effects of long-distance running on young girls, at that time so uncom-mon as to be uncharted. The doctor said I was fine, and I learned from the marathon that to finish a race you simply keep running; I learned to revel in the company of runners from around the world and the marvelous range of humanity standing in the streets to cheer everyone on, and to keep going until the finish line finds you.

I still loved the feeling of being out on a long run, feet pounding, arms pumping, thoughts slamming, miles and miles. Lightness came. Worry and struggle dissipated. Sometimes, for a flash, an insight or clarity would arrive, an answer to a question, a solution to a problem, or just a sudden wash of calm. It was a way of experiencing life that was different from my habitual goal- and achievement-oriented mindset. The feeling was more like the wonder I'd felt as a child, gazing at an oak tree, trans-fixed by the patterns of bark, the reassuring sense of company in listening to the rhythm of the cicadas' hum, or sitting still on the porch with my dog, Snoopy, his head resting in my lap, the warmth and peace and connection that traveled between us as real as the feel of my hand on his fur. How did these fleeting experiences work? What was happening in the mind? Why did these moments seem to dissolve worries and calm stress? Did everyone have these experiences? I wondered if these moments could be cultivated, or if they were inevitably and uncontrollably spontaneous.

My mentor in grad school, Dr. Martin Seligman, was the father of positive psychology and one of the first people in the field to show that we have a choice in how we build our inner lives, and how much this choice matters to our well-being. He found that much of our suffering is caused by habits of thought, and that we are most despairing when we perceive that we have no control over the outcome of a situation—when we think we can't control the link between our actions and the results. We might develop a pessimistic explanatory style, a negative and ultimately damaging way of telling our own story.

If I fail a test or my lover leaves me, I can explain the same event in different ways. If I'm using a pessimistic explanatory style, I respond to the bad grade or the breakup by saying, "I'm a loser." I tell the story of failure and loss as though it is internal (*I'm incompetent*), stable (*I'll never succeed in this subject or in a relationship*), and global (*I'm bad at everything*).

There is another way of explaining the same event that is external, unstable, and specific. Instead of labeling myself as flawed or incompetent, I could describe the external reality: "That test was really difficult" or "That relationship wasn't sustainable." Instead of deciding that I will continue to fail at tests and love and everything else, I could say, "I need to study harder in the future" or "I trust that the right person will come along someday."

Marty Seligman's impressive body of research showed that a pessimistic explanatory style carves a path to depression, while an optimistic explanatory style leads to resilience. In other words, we experience depression and other mental illnesses in part because we've learned to feel helpless in the face of circumstances that we wrongly believe are going to last forever, or are our fault, or the result of our damage or deficiency. Really, we have more control than we believe we do. Marty showed the therapeutic benefit of unlearning our false, negative beliefs, and choosing to see the world and ourselves differently. I wondered if this choice might have something to do with the buoyant, open, peaceful feeling I sometimes had when running or out in nature.

Marty and I would take long walks down Walnut Street in West Philadelphia in the summer, the academic season when thinking and research really get done, our ramble always ending with a cinnamon bun at his favorite bakery. We often discussed the choice we all have in controlling our cognition. We referred to harnessing this power as "the Apollonian state," after Apollo, the Greek god of the sun and light and truth. In the Apollonian state you could use reason to move away from despairing beliefs—*it's never going to change, it's all my fault, there must be something wrong with me*—and toward more empowered thinking.

I could remember being taught to cultivate this state as early as kindergarten, when I flew through the classroom door on the first day and sat, palms spread on the cool, smooth surface of my desk, waiting for my first *real life lesson*. The teacher greeted us and moved methodically through the room, placing an object on each student's desk. It was a thin book—a spiral-bound planner. She strode to the front of the room. "If you want to succeed," she said, her syllables clear and careful, "you must learn to manage your time." I took her lesson to heart. For all of high school I focused on getting good grades so I could get into college. In college, I pulled all-nighters. In grad school, if I slept at all, it was often on the floor, my face mashed against charts of statistical analysis. I wanted to be close to the work, to the numbers. I was ambitious, and just as with running, the drive to learn and suc-ceed served me well.

"But, Marty," I said one morning as we crossed the street and turned to walk back along a colorful block of narrow Victorian row houses, "could there be another beneficial inner state?" As I saw it, the Apollonian state was important, and could be healing. But it was still in the realm of control—having mastery, having self-control, moving pieces of life around.

I wondered if there might be another way of seeing reality, like the experience I had miles into a long run, that state of being when things are suddenly clear and unified, like being on a mountaintop and seeing the world from a new height and perspective. I told Marty that I thought of this state of mind as "the Olympian state"—like being on Mount Olympus, with a wide, unfettered, integrated view of the world rolling out in all directions. The value was less about feeling in control of circumstances, and more about glimpsing the world and life and purpose from a broader, more holistic view where the meaning and proportion of things becomes clear. When I felt this way, the usual stories—what I've accomplished, what I've lost, what I have—fell away like pickup sticks. A new narrative emerged. I felt inherently worthy and open to possibility and adventure, trusting that the world would reveal whatever I needed to know.

Was it possible that the patients at the makeshift Yom Kippur service on Unit 6 had reached something similar to the Olympian state? Rebecca's discovery of her wholeness and innocence, Sol's ability to bridge his extreme isolation—the shifts in all four patients that hadn't come from a drug or through talk therapy, but from what we had shared around the kitchen table.

Night was beginning to fall, the trees darkening to silhouettes. Phil hated if I ran alone past dusk, so I came out of the park at Columbus Circle and jogged the steps down to the subway to catch the B train home.

I joined the stream of tired passengers. The subway jerked and sped up. A murmur rose above the metallic squeal of the train. A devout man, a Lubavitcher with a black hat and full beard, was praying at the other end of the car. His eyes were closed, his face full of joy.

What inner mechanisms fueled his joy? Why, in a train packed with people who seemed so burdened and stressed, did this man appear so peaceful and free? It would take many years of research to begin to reveal any answers. But his face stayed in my mind. I was on the trail.

 CHAPTER 3

STARS IN A DARK SKY

In late December 1994, on the last day of my rotation on Unit 6, I humiliated myself by bursting into tears when I said goodbye to Mr. Danner at his outpatient appointment. "I'll always remember you," I told him, tears running down my cheeks. It was true. He'd touched me deeply. I didn't like that he'd dealt heroin or robbed people or risked giving his wife HIV. But I loved the part of him that was bigger than his wounds and wrongs, and it hurt to be in a system that cycled interns out of the same doors that patients kept reentering, all of us prevented from fostering long-term relationships and healing. He'd seemed angry at first when I told him I was leaving Unit 6, but when he saw my tears the storm left his eyes and he broke into a wide smile.

"Thank you," he said, still grinning as he left the room.

IN JANUARY I moved to my next rotation, working in a university student health service clinic. I anticipated that, in a clinic serving younger patients with less severe pathologies than on

Unit 6, the treatment model might be more innovative and less rigidly psychoanalytic, but once again I found that the trend was to delve into patients' pain without necessarily seeking to build their resilience or renewal; to treat them for six sessions and then refer them to psychiatrists for prescriptions and long-term care.

For some patients, that was appropriate. But of the forty or so patients I treated in six months, only a small percentage—maybe 15 or 20 percent—actually had the symptoms of major depressive disorder that warranted medication and psychiatric care. The others were depressed, but it was more existential in nature, not a bottomed-out depression but a sadness and disorientation accompanied by questions about meaning and purpose: *What's the point of life? Is there a larger meaning to existence? Why am I personally here?* These are painful questions to grapple with, but important ones, too, on the path of emerging adulthood.

They were the same questions I remembered asking when I was nineteen, a sophomore at Yale, reading Nietzsche deep in winter, surrounded by an academic culture that said there is no inherent meaning to life. I remember thinking, *What if that's true? What if there really is no meaning in the universe?* I fell into a depressive slump. I'd go down to the basement of my dorm, where there was a room that connected the underground hallways to different parts of campus. It was February and freezing cold, and I didn't know if God existed or if there was a purpose to my life. I'd sit by the water heater for warmth and go around and around in my head, afraid I'd never find the guidance I sought. My questions grew more and more bereft. *Is love even possible?* I wondered. *Is it even real? Will I feel joy again?*

When months passed and the slump didn't lift, I went to the campus health center for counseling, but each session just left me feeling even more depressed. The counselor dug for pain, just as I was later trained to do, seeing my questions not as authentic life-building questions, part of the process of individuating and becoming myself, but as symptoms of pathology. My questions weren't seen as valid questions that showed my authentic growth and hunger to know the nature of the world. They were seen as markers of some kind of violation against me as a child. Instead of validating my journey and inviting me back to my intuitive sense of the buoyancy and goodness of life, my counselor asked, "You say there is no meaning in life. Who is it who has broken your trust?"

I didn't know where to turn for guidance. I didn't trust myself. "For every question there are ten to fifty logical answers," I told my therapist one day. "How do you pick the one that is most true?" Now I understand what would have been a helpful response: "It sounds like you can argue both ways, yes and no, about whether there is meaning in life. Is there a part of you that has a deeply felt answer? Is there a time in the past when you accessed or authorized your inner knowing?" But she was stuck within a narrow, theoretically driven inquiry that didn't validate inner wisdom or multiple ways of knowing. And so she kept digging and circling for a childhood wound. I burrowed myself deeper and deeper into philosophical deconstruction. *If we change every minute, if our cells die and our ideas shift, can we say that we exist at all? Isn't any identity or meaning we perceive just a construction we invent and impose?*

That summer I landed in Washington, DC, for the internship that led me to Phil, and, in the sunlight and leafy green trees of Georgetown, the thoughts of my nihilist winter shook free and I landed back in the warmth of trusting myself. Joy spread in my chest again. I often laughed and smiled for no reason other than the pleasure of being. The good weather and the company of a boy I was growing to love had something to do with it. But sometimes a vestige of depression would reappear. Phil and I went to a pub one night where there was a photo on the wall from a hundred years ago. "None of the people in that photo are alive anymore," I said. "We're all going to die." It was a thought right out of the existential philosophy I'd been reading all winter. Phil cocked his head at me and then shuddered his arms as though shaking off cold mud. "Ugh," he said. "That could be the most needlessly morbid interpretation imaginable." *Right,* I realized. *We get to choose our stance.* We can use logic to arrive at answers, and rigorous thought does yield necessary information. We can also check in with our inner knowing and choose our guiding perspective on life.

I LEARNED SOMETHING useful in those dark winter days next to the water heater in the basement at Yale. Being with doubt and sadness, questioning what I believed, brought me beyond a one-track intellectual way of knowing the world, and into a felt awareness of life, which eventually returned me to a sense of buoyancy and belonging. I had to learn to give myself permission to trust my gut. Ultimately, I've come to realize, this has made me a better clinician, and also a better scientist.

When I returned to Yale in the fall, I didn't succumb to the fashionable deconstructionist attack on meaning. I sat in psychology classrooms learning taxonomies of symptoms and engaged in debates at tables full of philosophy majors, and asked myself, "What if there *is* deep meaning written into the universe? What if life holds an ultimate meaning? I haven't heard a single argument that disconfirms it."

When I began treating patients at the university student health clinic ten years after my own bout with depression, I made a pledge to validate the questions my patients were asking, and to help them do what they were trying to do: not sit in their pain, but build their lives. To navigate doubt and fear, and find a path to resilience and renewal.

A nineteen-year-old boy who grappled with anxiety came into my care. The prevailing psychoanalytic model would have had us exploring his childhood wounds, the ways he was mistreated and betrayed by his abusive father. Certainly, his current struggles had some connection with his past pain. But there's no bottom to the pain of an abusive parent. To make his therapy about living in that zone of mistreatment would have consigned him to the never-ending reliving of the hurt and anger and feelings of unworthiness. Instead, we stayed in the realm of the present. Right here and now, his main concern was about how to connect with the young women he was interested in. He didn't want to soak in the pain of his unhappy childhood. He wanted a girlfriend. So he brought in phone numbers and he practiced. By the end of his treatment, he was dating someone, and in their partnership he saw evidence of his kindness and worth. He felt hope for a better future, hope that he wouldn't go on to transmit the abusiveness he'd learned from his father.

Another patient, a twenty-year-old exchange student from Italy, came to the clinic because she was pregnant and needed support in figuring out what to do. My colleagues were surprised when I didn't automatically coach her to end the pregnancy and refer her to an abortion clinic. Instead, I stood by as witness to her trust in herself to find her own answer. This wasn't a decision for her parents, friends, doctors, or religious, cultural, or financial norms to make for her. I saw it as a fundamentally spiritual decision. No amount of advice or information could effectively guide her choice. She decided to keep the baby. I don't know what happened—whether she and the father, whom she loved, stayed together to raise the child; whether her family accepted or rejected her choice; whether she carried regrets or gratitude into her adulthood. I do know that when she came to her decision, she was working from within her deepest truth, and that my role wasn't to pathologize her thoughts or behaviors, or analyze her pain, but to listen with care and guide her in meeting and nurturing her emerging self.

At that time, in the mid-1990s, it was the trend to medicate patients through experiences of struggle and pain. The university student health center did not overmedicate. But they did overanalyze. When all you have is a hammer, everything is a nail. Psychologists were generally trained to see suffering, but not the emergence of a spiritual or existential journey. In search of mentors who could show me a different approach, I discovered the New York Center for Jungian Studies, where skilled practitioners with the same degrees I had were seeking to reintegrate a part of psychology that had been completely abandoned in our mainstream training and practice. The Jungians relied on dreams to reveal our wounds and emerging opportunities for healing; on archetypes to show universal human tendencies and developmental paths; and on synchronicity to explore our relationship to self and flow with life.

I remember attending a talk by a young man named Mark Kuras, who spoke about striving to guide patients beyond the individual conscious to discover the transcendent self, where we become windows to the collective unconscious. It made intuitive sense to me that we essentially live in two realms—the everyday world where we buy groceries and commute to work and bicker with our partners and watch the leaves change in the park; and the transcendent world that's bigger than any individual life, and to which we each belong.

At that point, what I knew about spiritual psychology amounted to the importance of building relationships and connection, the disservice of focusing exclusively on pathology and pain, and the possibility that healing comes both from discovering our inner wisdom and from the sudden glimpses of insight and meaning that can land precisely in our areas of greatest confusion or injury.

COMING OUT OF my clinical internship year in July 1995, I was awarded a three-year research postdoc funded by the National Institute of Mental Health, a grant that allowed me to study anything in the field of psychology. Suddenly I had forty or fifty quiet hours every week to pull and examine data, take a walk, get a coffee, and go back and gaze at the numbers again. I was looking at factors of resilience, using my colleague Myrna Weissman's beautifully designed data set to see if I could discern any patterns in factors that mitigate depression.

Myrna's data came from a fifteen-year longitudinal study she'd begun in 1980 at a depression clinic in New Haven, where she'd gathered participants and then matched them with non-depressed control subjects who were from the same neighborhood and shared other similar demographic variables. Considered a premier depression researcher in the country, Myrna had included all of the core variables the field used at the time to try to understand what increases our risk of or resilience against depression: Did the participant have a depressed mother? How had the participant been raised—with what kind of parenting style?

I was trying to filter and measure correlations among a vast range of data points. There were no algorithmic menus in those days to sort the data—I had to write and code the equations by hand, using a kind of statistical modeling called regression analysis, a process for examining the relationships between multiple variables. A regression is a formula that allows you to look at the relative contributions of multiple variables on a single variable, for example: A + B + C + D = X. In my research, the single variable X was childhood depression. I wanted to know what factors of personality, upbringing, and personal and family history contribute to a child experiencing depression. In multivariate linear regression, you can say that the degree to which you have A, the degree to which you have B, the degree to which you have C, and the degree to which you have D together culminate in the extent to which you have X. And you can look at the unique impact of variable A by paring away all its overlap with B, C, and D, and the unique impact of variable B by paring away its overlap with A, C, and D, and so on.

I'd write out an equation to test the impact of a combination of variables, and then wait for the computer to process and print out the results. Each time, I'd almost hold my breath, excited to pore over the results. I often worked all day, lost track of time, and raced home to meet Phil for dinner. During dinner, my mind would wander back to the data. Phil would bang on the table. "Hello, what are you thinking about?" he'd say, exasperated. "Are you thinking about your equations?"

I was always thinking about numbers. And soon they began to light up in jaw-dropping patterns, like constellations emerging from a dark sky. The effect of maternal depression on childhood depression: a twofold increased risk. The effect of poverty on depression: a 40 percent increase associated with the variable "a problem paying bills." The effect of parenting style on depression: when a parent, father or mother, is affectionate but not overly controlling, a child's risk for depression is cut by 18 to 30 percent.

This resilience data was fascinating and useful. But what I really wanted to understand was what had happened in the back kitchen at Yom Kippur. What *was* that healing lift, and what variables could I use to measure how spiritual experiences relate to depression? My colleagues told me they couldn't think of anything in the data sets related to religion or spirituality. But then the data manager lifted her head at a meeting one day and said, "No, I think we do have something you can use." She pointed to two questions hidden at the back of the eighty-page structured diagnostic interviews:

1. How personally important is religion or spirituality to you (highly important; moderately important; somewhat important; not important)?
2. How frequently do you attend religious service (once a week or more; at least once a month; several times a year; very rarely)?

The original purpose of the questions seemed more to measure participants' diversity than to discover the impact of spirituality on their health and experience. But at least the questions were there, a resource waiting to be brought forward. Using gold-standard statistical approaches and one of the field's most trusted and well-developed data sets, I could investigate how participants' responses to these two spirituality-related questions corresponded with other variables, and see whether there was any pattern to describe the relationship between their spirituality and their mental health and well-being.

In those days, we could only access the data in person, sitting in the medical school. I started working sixty-hour weeks, getting up early on the weekends to go for a run and then heading to my office to analyze the numbers. One Sunday morning, I left Phil lazing at home with the newspaper to spend the day with my equations. It was midsummer and the platform to the 1/9 uptown train was crowded and boiling hot. Minutes ticked by, and several times trains rolled in, the crowd pressed forward in the damp heat, and then the trains rolled on through without stopping. When a packed train finally stopped, I was surprised to see one car toward the back of the train that was nearly empty, and I headed toward it. As I settled in, congratulating myself on having landed a seat, I realized that the car only appeared half-empty because the passengers were all slammed together at the far end of the car.

On my side of the car there was a disheveled and distressed man yelling at the other passengers. "Hey, you want to come sit with me?" he'd holler across the car. As passengers boarded at the next stop, he yelled to each one, "Hey, you want to sit with me?" They whipped their heads away from him and bolted toward the mass of passengers at the far end of the car. It was the same at 96th Street and 103rd Street. When no one acknowledged him, the man grew increasingly agitated.

"Hey, you want some of my lunch?" he called. When the only response was stony silence, he started throwing pieces of chicken across the car. "You want some of my lunch?" he yelled, picking meat off the bones and throwing it. When the bones were clean, he started throwing the bones, still yelling, "Hey, you want some lunch?"

He carried on like this up to 110th Street, 116th Street, 125th Street. At 145th Street the train stopped and the door opened and the most elegant duo stood poised on the platform ready to board, a grandmother in a green pastel dress and pillbox hat, a little girl in pink, both wearing beautiful white gloves. I could feel the other passengers freeze as though in dread of the moment when a piece of meat or bone would land on their immaculate church clothes.

Sure enough, the man craned his neck toward them and yelled at the top of his voice, "Hey, you want to come sit with me?" He pointed right at them. The grandmother and granddaughter looked at each other squarely, nodded, and marched right over to him and sat down on the shiny orange seats, hands in their laps, backs straight, eyes ahead. He looked at them, stunned. "Hey, do you want some of my lunch?" he asked, and whipped out another piece of chicken. They looked at each other, nodded, and turned to him, saying in unison, "No, thank you." "Are you sure you don't want some?" he asked. The grandmother and granddaughter were calm as they politely turned to him again and said, "No, thank you."

It dawned on me that I was witnessing the passing of a torch from older generation to younger—a deliberate sensibility and way of being in the world, a way of relating to others. Maybe because they were dressed for church, I thought of the Bible verse in Matthew that says, "Whatever you did for one of the least of these brothers and sisters of mine, you did for me." The grandmother and granddaughter were living this spiritual sensibility, and it was so integrated in their approach to life that they didn't even need words to communicate it.

When I got to the Columbia medical school and returned to the data, the grandmother and granddaughter were still on my mind. I wondered if I could measure what I'd seen in the subway car—what seemed like the passing of a spiritual torch. And if intergenerational transmission of spirituality could be identified, what was its impact on depression?

I ran some equations using another kind of modeling, drawing on mother-child matches, trying different combinations—a mother who was high or not-high in spirituality paired with a child who was high or not-high in spirituality, with depression or no-depression. I discovered something striking: when the mother and child were both high in spirituality, the child was 80 percent protected against depression, compared with mothers and children who were not concordant for spirituality, or mothers and children who were not high in spirituality. In other words, a child was five times less likely to be depressed when spiritual life was shared with a mother. The spiritual bond I'd witnessed between the grandmother and granddaughter on the train carried the antidote to depression. This was true whether the child was at high or low risk of depression. While maternal depression doubled the risk for depression in the child, the five-fold protective benefit of spirituality I'd uncovered meant that spirituality matters twice as much to our mental health as maternal mental health.

Even when I added in all the variables that mainstream clinical science had shown are linked to childhood depression—mother's depression, poverty, a stormy home environment, overly cold or controlling parenting—I found that intergenerational transmission of spirituality held the same astounding 80 percent protective benefit. It was the largest protective effect I'd seen anywhere in the resilience literature.

So much of science is a step-by-step chipping away. Testing a theory. Following the numbers. Every so often, there's a blasting light so strong, it's like the beam from a lighthouse hitting your face, so clear and shocking that it takes your breath away. Something about the intergenerational transmission of spirituality created the kind of soil and environment where the seeds of depression were unlikely to sprout and take root. The thrilling, blinding light of this truth was so powerful that I couldn't wait to follow it for the rest of my career.

CHAPTER 4

TWO SIDES OF THE SAME COIN

published the finding on intergenerational transmission of spirituality in the *Journal of the American Academy of Child and Adolescent Psychiatry*—called "the orange journal" for its colored cover, the best science journal on children's mental health—and the paper won a Templeton Prize for scientific and spiritual curiosity. But even these rigorous validations of the science and acknowledgment of the significance of the finding didn't advance the conversation around the relationship between spirituality and mental health. If anything, the silence became more deafening. Some of my colleagues would ask, "Yes, but is what you're investigating really *psychology?*" They seemed to view spirituality as a cultural or institutional artifact, not as I was coming to see it: as a way of being in the world.

Then, one spring morning in 1997, only a few months after my article had been published, I was skimming the most recent issue of *The American Journal of Psychiatry* while Phil and I hurried through breakfast. He had quit his corporate law job and started commuting to Connecticut to work at a tiny, innovative hedge fund run out of his mentor's home office, exchanging the beehive of elevators and impersonal glass skyscrapers for a carpeted room with comfy peach-colored chairs in a little white house. Before he'd changed jobs, it had seemed he was getting from one minute to the next by going through the motions. He hadn't complained, but I'd seen his unhappiness leaking out in his resistance to getting out of bed in the morning, in the strange color combinations he often chose from his closet full of meticulously curated office suits. When he wore a black jacket with blue pants I wondered if there was a hint of rebelliousness in his deviation from "the uniform," or if it was entirely a carelessness born of exhaustion. Now he seemed more engaged and at ease. I took a slug of coffee, and then saw an article headline so surprising I almost spit out my sip. "Religion, Psychopathology, and Substance Use and Abuse: A Multimeasure, Genetic-Epidemiologic Study." Dr. Kenneth Kendler, a foremost leader in psychiatric-epidemiology in twin studies, had published a study on the relationship between religion, spirituality, and various psychiatric symptoms. It was fresh research from a well-regarded lab—and, other than my own recent study, the first article I'd found anywhere in the scientific literature that examined the intersection between spirituality and mental health.

Studies of twins are something of a gold standard in scientific research because they allow us to investigate which traits are more influenced by genes or by environment. While they don't help us identify exact one-to-one correlations of a specific gene or combination of genes to a trait or diagnosis, they do give us a big-picture view of the broad heritability of a trait or condition.

To determine whether a trait is inborn or socialized or a blend of the two, scientists look for statistical patterns of personality traits, medical conditions, or mental health diagnoses across the twin pairs. For example, if one twin has major depression, what is the likelihood the other twin is also depressed? If a twin has a particular IQ score, what are the odds the other twin has the same IQ? If one twin is outgoing and extroverted, what are the chances that the other twin is too?

Then the researcher determines to what degree the patterns of trait similarity are based on genetic similarity. For example, identical twins share nearly 100 percent of their genetic material, whereas fraternal twins, like any other sibling pair, share just 50 percent. By comparing how similar identical twins Jennifer and Jessica are to how similar fraternal twins Abby and Sarah are, we can figure out the factor by which shared genetic material contributes to trait similarity.

We can also figure out the degree of similarity between twins as a function of the environment they share. For example, some twins are separated at birth and adopted into or raised by different families; some have parents who divorce, and one parent raises one twin while the other parent raises the other. If Jennifer and Jessica share 100 percent of their genetic material but grew up in different homes, what is the impact of their different home environment on their personality traits and medical and mental health diagnoses? What about for Abby and Sarah, who share 50 percent of their genetic material and grew up in the same home?

Of course, our environments change as we get older. Twins raised in the same house come of age, graduate from high school, and often go on to live in different environments—attending different colleges, pursuing different professions, forming new relationships and families. Some of the statistical analysis in twin studies examines the impact of genes versus environment—and further statistical modeling looks at the influence of shared versus unique environments.

In this new study, Dr. Kendler examined the genetic versus environmental basis for spirituality. With his colleagues at Virginia Commonwealth University, he had conducted personal assessments with 1,902 twins from female-female pairs—some identical twins, some fraternal—in the Virginia Twin Registry, a database of every twin born in the state of Virginia over two decades. He then applied statistical models to the data to determine the extent to which the participants' spirituality was linked to genetic or environmental factors, and to see if there were any documentable effects of spirituality on the participants' psychological health.

There wasn't time to finish reading the article at home, so I brought it with me to work. The results of the study were striking.

Dr. Kendler established a clear distinction between personal spirituality and strict adherence to the rule of religion, or what Kendler called "personal conservatism." In his largely Judeo-Christian sample, personal spirituality measured items such as "frequency of seeking spiritual comfort" and "frequency of private prayer," while personal conservatism measured items such as "belief that God rewards and punishes" and "literal belief in the Bible." Kendler found that personal devotion and personal conservatism go hand in hand for some people, but not the majority of those studied. Following a particular religious text very closely didn't necessarily mean or not mean that a person reported a felt sense of being in a personal relationship with a higher power, or turning to a higher power or source for guidance in times of difficulty. In other words, a person could measure high in personal devotion while anywhere from high to low in personal conservatism, and vice versa. Kendler's research was the first major empirical study supporting the important distinction that people can be spiritual with or without being religious, and religious with or without being spiritual.

The study's next set of findings was even more significant.

Kendler showed three vital and heretofore unexplored correlations between spirituality and mental health.

First, low levels of depressive symptoms are related to high levels of personal devotion. That is, if you have a high degree of spirituality, you're less likely to be depressed.

Second, Kendler found that personal devotion can serve as a buffer against the negative psychological effects of stressful life events such as illness, divorce, or loss of a loved one. Interestingly, when viewed minus the presence or absence of personal devotion, personal conservatism—or religious practice—didn't have the same buffering effect. Personal devotion—a sense of personal relationship with a higher power—was the active ingredient that carried the protective benefit, with or without personal conservatism.

Third, he found that personal devotion decreased the lifetime risk for alcoholism and nicotine dependence. Spiritual people are less likely to be addicted. The findings showed correlation, not causation, but it was a start in revealing the effects of spirituality on our mental health.

And then I read the greatest breakthrough in Dr. Kendler's study.

In twin studies, we don't get exact one-to-one correlations of a specific gene or combination of genes to a trait or diagnosis, but we get a big-picture view of a trait or diagnosis's broad heritability. At this point, twin studies had been applied to IQ, to most forms of mental illness (depression, anxiety, substance abuse, schizophrenia, bipolar disorder), and to the "big five" personality traits: openness to experience, conscientiousness, extroversion, agreeableness, and neuroticism. Kendler's innovation was to apply standard twin-study statistical modeling to measure the degree to which spirituality is innate or socialized.

He found that there is a significant genetic contribution to spirituality. Specifically, our capacity for a personal spiritual life is *29 percent heritable*. In other words, when we look at human variance in spirituality, a person's degree of spirituality is determined 29 percent by heredity, and 71 percent by environment. Our spirituality is substantially—roughly two-thirds—a factor of how we're raised, the company we keep, the things we do to build the muscle. But still a significant degree of our capacity to experience the sacred and transcendent—one-third—is inscribed in our genetic code, as innate as our eye color or fingerprints.

No clinical scientist had ever published findings on spirituality as an innate capacity—as a human attribute that could have heritable as well as socialized components. Up until then, spirituality had been seen in the eyes of clinical science as synonymous with religion, and understood as a belief, a set of views, a choice, perhaps a crutch to rely on in hard times—not as an aspect of human experience that might be core to our innate being. Kendler's study was the first time that the scientific community had published research exploring the possibility that there might be a genetic capacity within us for spiritual experience.

The new research raised the possibility that just as we are cognitive, physical, and emotional beings, we are also spiritual beings. In other words, it's possible that we are built to be spiritual and that spirituality might be a fundamental and necessary part of our human inheritance that contributes to our mental health. Kendler's groundbreaking study suggested that spirituality isn't just a belief, but something each of us is born with the capacity to experience. Like any innate capacity—the ability to learn a language or sing a tune, for example—there is variability in its strength. Some people are more genetically inclined to play an instrument or do calculus. But ultimately, the ability to be spiritual is our birthright.

When I finished reading the article in my office at Columbia, I carefully tore out the pages of Kendler's study and put them in my purse, a reminder that science could be a lens to investigate my deepest questions and behold potential answers.

KENDLER AND I had been working on our studies at the same time, unaware of each other, and now we had published complementary findings. The grandmother and granddaughter on the train had led me to a discovery of the protective benefits of intergenerational transmission of spirituality. And Kendler contributed the genetic, epidemiological evidence establishing that spirituality is an innate and foundational way of being. The inner capacity that allowed the grandmother and granddaughter to see the distraught and disheveled man throwing chicken on the train as more than an intrusive presence in dirty jeans is a deeply human capacity for which we're hardwired—and that can be cultivated. Both Kendler and I had discovered, through different methodologies and among different data sets, that when we cultivate this innate capacity for personal spirituality, we are protected against depression.

I wrote to him in excitement over the shared terrain of our research. *Your article is breathtaking,* I wrote. I told him I'd been looking at spirituality as a resilience factor among children and teenagers, and asked if I could replicate some of his methodology and examine the effects and protective benefits of personal spirituality in a younger sample. *If spirituality is an innate capacity,* I wrote, *then it has to develop. I'd like to study how.*

He wrote back, enthusiastic about my project, and encouraged me to reach out to Dr. Ronald Kessler, a senior scientist at Harvard Medical School, who had headed up a team that built an impressive data set of adolescents from the National Comorbidity Survey, the first nationally representative mental health survey in the United States. The National Comorbidity Survey itself had resulted in notable findings. It showed that only 20 percent of the people who had experienced a mental health disorder in the past year had received professional help, for example. Now the data from the National Comorbidity Survey was helping researchers to analyze other large-scale implications of mental health.

Using Kendler's newly established variables of personal devotion (as partially hardwired) and personal conservatism (as nearly entirely socialized) on Kessler's large, randomly selected sample of adolescents aged thirteen to nineteen, I began investigating the relationship between personal spirituality and various markers of mental health. The mean age in Kendler's study had been thirty-one. In looking at similar questions and correlations in a younger sample, I was essentially investigating the developmental antecedent to what Kendler had found among adults, putting the lens of science up to spiritual growth formation in teens.

Before Kendler's 1997 paper, no one in psychology had disentangled spirituality from religion. He was the first to show that while religion can support a person's spiritual life, religion and spirituality are distinct. While personal spirituality may be practiced within a faith tradition, it includes a deeply felt and perceived connection with a higher power or a sacred world—a sense of engagement and relationship, such as asking God or Source for guidance in times of struggle. Kendler had shown that adults make a clear distinction between religion and spirituality, and that the protective benefits come from personal spirituality. I wondered if the same was true for adolescents, and what the data might suggest about the formation of spiritual identity.

I found that for young people spirituality and religion are

distinct, but not as distinct as they are for adults. Personal devotion and personal conservatism correlate more closely in adolescents (by a degree of 0.3) than in Kendler's adults (by a degree
of 0.1), suggesting that there's an individuation process through
which religion and personal spirituality get disentangled. No
matter what faith tradition we're raised in, and whether or not
we're raised in a faith tradition, part of our human development
involves discerning what we agree and disagree with and finding
our own personal seat of spiritual awareness. For Kendler's adults,
this process was complete. For the teens in Kessler's data set, this
work of individuation was still in progress.

Remarkably, I found that in the nationally representative
sample of teens, adolescents with a strong personal spirituality
were *35 to 75 percent* less likely to experience clinical depression.
Kendler had also found a correlation between spirituality and
mental health in adults—but my study showed spirituality to be
even more robustly protective—*nearly twice as protective*—in teens.
No other mental health intervention, clinical or pharmacological, for adults or adolescents, had anything close to these prevention rates. And the protective benefit was most powerful right in
the window of risk when we are most likely to get stuck with a
first episode of depression. The opportunity for highly protective spiritual emergence coexisted with developmental risk for
depression. In other words, spirituality had a more pronounced
advantage for teenagers who were in the typical window when
mental health issues emerge. People who were at greater risk for
mental illness due to their developmental stage actually had the
most to gain from spirituality.

I found that the process of spiritual individuation impacted
resilience in other ways as well. For example, adolescents with a
strong personal spirituality were *40 to 80 percent* less likely to

develop substance dependence or abuse. This was a shocking scale of magnitude. I didn't know of any other preventive or treatment model that showed anywhere close to a similar result.

I wondered if the opposite could be true—if the ballooning of addiction and depression in adolescence could be a sign of spiritual struggle. I thought back to my own depression in college, and to the students I'd worked with in the university health center who came in searching for ultimate meaning and direction but were treated only at the symptom level, not in their process of spiritual emergence. What if the elevated rates of addiction and depression we saw in teens were because young people were struggling to form spiritually and we weren't supporting them?

Was it possible that the same piece of our genetic wiring carried both the risk for depression *and* the capacity to be spiritually aware? That depression and spirituality might really be opposite sides of the same coin? Might they even share a common physiology? What if the condition we pathologize and diagnose as depression is sometimes actually spiritual hunger—a normal and genetically derived part of human development that is unhealthy to muffle or deny?

CHAPTER 5

SOMEONE WATCHING OVER ME

A year or so into my National Institute of Mental Health–funded postdoc, I asked if I could see patients in Columbia Presbyterian's outpatient Children's Anxiety and Depression Clinic. Working with the numbers had afforded me a breathtaking view of resilience in adolescence—but I wanted to explore how our field might apply the findings to support the growth and development of living, breathing young people.

The clinic was on the seventh floor of a huge building on West 168th Street, off Broadway. Like the hospital that housed Unit 6, Columbia Presbyterian was an old urban hospital building with slow elevators and drab hallways. But while the previous hospital felt integrated into the neighborhood, Columbia Presbyterian rose up stark and imposing along Riverside Drive and the wide current of the Hudson. We served the communities of Harlem and Washington Heights. The children we treated were grappling daily with poverty, loss, and difficult home environments. A number of families had recently moved from Haiti or the Dominican Republic. Many patients carried legacies of trauma or abuse. In addition to treating depressed and anxious children and adolescents, I was researching the dynamic of resilience, looking for treatment models that helped even the most vulnerable kids thrive despite their challenging circumstances. Soon patients like Iliana, a thirteen-year-old struggling with major depression, were leading me toward new insights about the relationship between spirituality and mental wellness.

When I met Iliana in the waiting room on her first visit to the clinic, she stood out right away in the room full of family groups, mostly mothers or grandmothers and young children clustered together, waiting on blue vinyl chairs. She had come alone. She was wearing jeans and a short red jacket and sat hunched with her arms crossed, her long dark hair half covering her face. I could sense her sadness and isolation even before she spoke.

In my office, Iliana took a seat in a sterile-looking chair with lacquered wood armrests. She seemed so small and rigid, with one arm pulled tightly across her body, gripping the opposite elbow with her hand. Her upper back was rounded, her chest sunken in, as though to form a shield around her heart.

She spoke first, staring at the floor, her words quick and direct. "My father died," she said. "He had a deli on 194th. Two guys came in. He knew them—he thought they were his friends. But they were high. They robbed him, and then they shot him."

Tears fell as she spoke. Her dark eyes seemed hollow with sorrow. In my work I'd seen depression usually present in one of two ways: someone either becoming so remote and withdrawn that they almost disappeared, or the depression surfacing as anxiety and tension. Iliana was more anxious than remote. Her whole body was wound tight, her sadness wrapped around her like a shroud. Even so, I could detect a fierce strength in her core. Every once in a while, she shot a look at me as though checking my reaction, making sure I was still following her, as if assessing whether or not I would be able to throw her the lifeline she was urgently seeking.

"My mom's an addict. Her boyfriend's a dealer. I used to live with my father," she continued, "but I live with my mother and grandmother now. My grandmother is very strict, and my mom is barely home."

She wasn't allowed to leave their apartment in Washington Heights except to go to school. In her warm, communal neighborhood the kids would go out at night and visit on the stoops of their buildings. But her grandmother had forbidden her to join them. Feeling trapped and under siege in the apartment, Iliana had barricaded herself in her room, pushing her dresser in front of the door to keep her mother and grandmother from entering. They had given up trying to get her to come out. She said she used to be a happy person with lots of friends, but in the three months since she'd lost her father, Horatio, whom she loved more than anyone, she had become a different person. She cried all day at school, and cried all night alone in her room. Her teacher had noticed the sudden change and advised her to see the school guidance counselor. Because the school was in the catchment area of Columbia Presbyterian, the counselor had referred her to our clinic.

Iliana had shown incredible courage and resilience in seeking help, but when I used the clinic's standard screener to assess her symptoms of depression—such as determining whether or not she was eating and sleeping well, if she had bouts of uncontrollable crying or lethargy, if she experienced feelings of hopelessness or unworthiness—I could see that her situation was dire. The higher the score on the screener, the more severe the symptoms. A score of 10 to 12 raises concern. On her first visit, Iliana scored 27.

Iliana began to see me every Tuesday without fail, but as the weeks passed, she continued to score distressingly high on the depression screener, dipping slightly but never scoring lower than 20. The two primary therapies we used at the clinic—cognitive behavioral therapy and interpersonal therapy—while very effective for some patients, didn't seem to be helping her.

Cognitive behavioral therapy (CBT), the most lauded technique of the day, and the primary method taught in top graduate schools, holds that our anxiety and suffering come from our misguided thoughts and how we relate to them. We all have habitual ways of thinking that help us in ordering our sense of reality. When we're experiencing depression or anxiety, our habitual ways of perceiving and thinking are often askew, and in CBT we try to free patients from those distorted thoughts and schemas. The therapist's job in CBT is to listen for the patient's pattern of dysfunctional thoughts and identify the underlying core schema (*my mother doesn't love me; I'm unsafe*), and then work to dismantle the misguided beliefs that are causing the suffering. This modality of treatment can be very helpful, particularly when the patient's suffering comes from damaging mental processes such as panic attacks or phobias, or from self-disparaging or helpless forms of depression. But Iliana's pain came from a deep grief and an untenable home dynamic—from recent traumatic loss, not from a misguided way of thinking about herself or the world. I tried searching for some kind of underlying distorted view that could be harming her, but the same core truth emerged: she had lost her father, and her heart was broken.

Interpersonal psychotherapy (IPT), the other structured therapy we practiced at the clinic, is based on the premise that social support saves the day—that regardless of its causes, depression can be treated through renegotiating our social context and finding better mentors and guides. In young patients, IPT often helps by accelerating adolescent individuation—helping young people learn the skills to advocate for themselves and avail themselves of resources. But Iliana was already doing that. She'd gone to the school guidance counselor, and then to the clinic, and back to see me each week, all on her own. She was a remarkable self-advocate. But the one relationship that was most important to her—the one with her father—had been cut short. Her father had been the sun in her life. Now he was gone, and the world had gone dark and cold. Her strict grandmother and absentee mother only made the world colder, and no amount of resources or helpful adults would bring back his light.

SOMETIMES ILIANA BROUGHT in elaborate collages she'd made by pasting pictures of teenage rock idols onto a big sheet of white cardboard.

"Look at him," she'd say, pointing to one of the teenage singers on her poster. "He looks so sweet, doesn't he? He looks so kind."

She wasn't allowed to speak to boys, much less go to parties, but she was curious about both. She was like a princess in a tower, separate and fortressed and hungry to connect, using images to try to access the social world she'd been denied.

This was the arena where IPT might help her. She couldn't bring her father back, but maybe she could find a way to renegotiate the relationships in her current family situation, to reorganize her world so that she was less barricaded. Maybe she could move the dresser, or even crack her door open a little, let in some light.

Given the harsh climate at home, I wanted to make sure Iliana had as much support as possible as she worked to alter the family dynamic, and so, with her consent, I invited her mother and grandmother to join us for her fifth session. I wasn't sure they would come. But on Tuesday when I went to the waiting room to get Iliana, there they were, sitting beside her in the blue vinyl chairs. The grandmother, an immigrant from the Dominican Republic, wore a pressed white blouse and long fitted skirt. Her dark graying hair was pulled back in a tight bun, the tracks of the comb still visible. She sat straight as a rod, her handbag held stiffly in her lap.

Iliana's mother was dressed more casually, in jeans and tennis shoes and a worn nightclub jacket with shoulder pads and tapered sleeves. Her hair hung loose to her shoulders. She wasn't disheveled, but she seemed distant and disconnected. She avoided eye contact, rarely letting her gaze land before it slid away again. She was in her mid-thirties, but looked less like a parental figure and more like a teenager who'd been called out for a transgression. I had the strong sense that the grandmother had made her come.

The grandmother and mother wanted to speak to me alone first, without Iliana, and in my office began to express their sadness and worry.

"Iliana is so angry, she won't come out of her room," the grandmother said. "She blocks the door. She's mad that I won't let her go out. But she's thirteen, she's beginning to look like a woman. I don't want her at parties." She gave me a pointed look. "I don't want her to end up like her mother."

Iliana's mother sat still. She didn't appear offended or surprised. It seemed as though they'd been through this drill before. Her only reaction to her mother's criticism was to glance at me, not asking for my help, but as if to say, "That's the truth. This is our story."

I turned to Iliana's grandmother. "You want very much to keep Iliana safe."

Her back straightened and her jaw tensed. She nodded.

"You're afraid if you let her go out to parties, then anything could happen."

For an instant, her guardedness fell away. Her face looked open. "I have to tell you something," she said, leaning forward ever so slightly. She took a quick, shallow breath. "I was sexually abused when I was a child. Then again when I was a teenager." She pointed at Iliana's mother. "My daughter, she was also abused."

Both women looked directly at me. Iliana's mother nodded.

"We know how bad it can be," the grandmother continued.

Beneath the grandmother's stony fortress and the mother's disengagement were tender, pained hearts trying to protect a little girl. But their good intentions were unfolding in a way that was harming Iliana, not helping her. I spoke softly. "Does Iliana know about the abuse you experienced?"

"We never told her," the grandmother said. "We want you to tell her. Here. Today."

They went back to the waiting room, and Iliana came into my office alone.

When I told her the hard truth her grandmother had asked me to share, she looked down at the floor. She said nothing for a few minutes. Her burdened hunch slowly relaxed into a soft slump, and when at last she lifted her head there were tears on her cheeks. "It's so sad," she said. "It just makes me so sad they had to go through that."

Even in her own suffering she could feel theirs acutely. She also seemed a little disoriented, as though what she'd just learned had forced her to put the world together in a new way.

WITH THE PAINFUL secret out in the open, things began to im-prove. It was nothing like the surprising big blast I'd witnessed at our Yom Kippur service on the inpatient unit, a sudden mental reset that brought fresh awareness and orientation and seemed to spontaneously move the patients from cognition of guilt and low self-esteem to a sense of worthiness and generosity. Iliana's healing was important, but different. It was step by step, by the book. Slowly, incrementally, Iliana's anxiety eased. The rigidity left her body. She didn't grasp her elbow anymore as though warding off an impending attack. She began eating meals at the kitchen table with her grandmother. She moved the dresser away from her bedroom door. Her grandmother finally agreed to let her hang out with her friends on the stoop.

But her sadness intensified. She slumped lower and lower in her chair, her back rounded, her eyes sunken and sullen. She had entered therapy with two problems: her intense grief, and the disconnected, barracked world at home. Her walled-off world had opened up. But there was still the gaping void of loss.

On the six-month anniversary of her father's death, her father's mother held a traditional Dominican ceremony to honor and reconnect with his spirit, ask for his blessing, and support his transition to heaven. Iliana seemed a little brighter the week after the ceremony. But her scores on the depression screener remained very high. They had dropped from the initial 27, only to remain plateaued around 16 to 18. The positive changes at home and in her social world weren't touching the vast emptiness left by her father's death. I worried that we'd reached the limits of what the standard treatment models could do to improve her mental health.

Then my young patient found her own cure.

A COUPLE OF WEEKS after the ceremony at her grandmother's home, she came to her Tuesday appointment as though transformed, completely energized and glowing.

"Guess what happened, Dr. Miller!" she exclaimed. "Guess!"

She'd been allowed to go to a dance at her middle school—the first organized social event that she'd been permitted to attend—provided that she was chaperoned at every moment by two older cousins. And at the dance she'd met a boy.

"He danced with me, he talked with me for a long time! He was so polite and nice and sweet! But that's not the best part. Guess what his name is!"

Horatio, she told me. The same name as her deceased father.

I leaned forward, curious to hear what she made of the strange confluence.

"It's a sign!" she said. "Don't you see? My father is watching over me. My father sent him."

For months and months, she had been suffering, empty and alone. All of a sudden, she was buoyant and connected, as though a part of her that had been shuttered was now opened up, a dark corner illuminated. The change was so palpable, so extreme, it took my breath away.

I was even more shocked when I assessed her on the depression screener that I'd been using to track her progress since the beginning of her treatment. For the first time since she'd begun treatment, Iliana's score fell to a low, single-digit 5. Her significant symptoms of extreme depression were largely gone.

She had met a kind boy who in her mind proved two things: boys weren't all scary or abusive or off-limits to her; and her father was protecting her. The thread of warmth and joyful relationship she'd had with him was still alive, despite the fact that he was dead. Her father walked with her. She wasn't alone.

THE TWENTIETH-CENTURY CLINICAL treatment models I'd been trained to use would all have said that in meeting the boy

Horatio, Iliana had experienced no more than a surprising co-incidence. That to heal properly, she needed to work through her grief and accept that her father was gone. But Iliana whole-heartedly perceived that, through Horatio, her father had sent her a message that he was looking out for her, that it was safe to rejoin the world of the living. As time went on, though she didn't stay in contact with the boy Horatio, she never wavered from the conviction that her father was protecting her.

In the weeks and months to come, Iliana continued to score very low on the mental health screener, experiencing few to nearly no symptoms of depression. Her chatty, quick, happy, light personality reemerged.

Iliana continued to attribute her recovery to the experience at the dance, when she had felt a mystical, direct awareness of her father's spirit. I wondered if the Dominican ceremony her grandmother had held to mark her father's passing had also been part of the perceptual breakthrough, allowing Iliana to move from alone to held, from bereft to cherished. Had the ceremony somehow opened her up to the experience at the dance, help-ing her to notice and be alert to the possible meaning of the spontaneous meeting with a boy named Horatio? However it had happened, Iliana had experienced a kind of interpersonal therapy—except the relationship she had renegotiated was with a person who was dead.

I wrestled with what to do to support Iliana. Might it be dan-gerous for her to believe in an ongoing relationship with her deceased father? Was Iliana's perception of her father's interces-sion in her life delusional? Might it prevent her from accepting the reality of his death? A strictly psychoanalytic treatment model would interpret her deep inner knowing of her deceased father's continued presence in her life as a wish or fantasy, and interpret what had happened—that the only boy she'd spoken to in a meaningful way shared her dead father's unusual name—as nothing more than a random event, however coincidental, to which she'd imputed meaning. I thought back to my own dark winter at Yale, how I'd questioned the meaning of life and my own sense of identity and purpose. Iliana, through the darkness of isolation and grief, had found her way to a sense of meaning and connection. She was no longer alone. Her father wasn't lost, he was with her, and she felt protected, guided, loved. If I had used a classical psychoanalytic treatment approach, I'd have risked harming her in two ways: by invalidating both her inner knowing and her perception that the world is full of meaning.

When I met Iliana, she had seen her life only through the framework of loss and isolation. She was stuck and alone, powerless to bring her father back, powerless to alter her mother's absence and addiction, powerless to protect her mother and grandmother from the abuse they'd suffered. No amount of self-advocacy could erase that suffering, and her powerlessness felt oppressive and imprisoning. But now she had shifted lenses. All on her own, she had fundamentally changed the way she perceived the same realities and circumstances. She had achieved a bigger view, an understanding that even in her suffering she was safe and held. She had witnessed that even in times of pain and grief, even at the worst and darkest moments, something in the fabric of the world allows for love and light.

As a clinician, I was glad that Illiana had achieved and sustained such an improved state of well-being. And as a scientist, I wondered what had really caused her to move from one framework to the other. Could others use the same mental shift to heal, and could it be done consciously, intentionally?

I shared my questions with one of my clinical supervisors and she unequivocally shook her head. "It was very nice of you to regard her experience as important," she said. "The spirituality we see among this population is a common part of the patients' culture and relative lack of education. It's something we need to respect as part of their diversity. They still have diagnostic mental illness."

Even without the trauma of her father's death, life had set Iliana up for depression. She was a girl in puberty, already a huge risk factor. Her mother and grandmother were both survivors of sexual abuse, which meant she was ripe to inherit that legacy of trauma. Her depression had indeed been severe, almost off the charts. And yet she had made a remarkable recovery, and during the months that I continued to work with her, Iliana's symptoms were reliably and significantly diminished.

She was a case study of risk and resilience, and her story illustrated in human terms what my epidemiological science was showing: that personal spirituality was a significant factor in mental health that warranted further investigation; and that there was a strong relationship between a person's risk for depression and potential to benefit from spirituality.

YET THE STRONG correlations between spirituality and mental health that I'd seen in Kenneth Kendler's study, and in my own epidemiological research and clinical work, were still largely invisible in the field.

In 1998, two years after I'd met Iliana, I received an unexpected opportunity to bring the inquiry forward in an important forum. Columbia hosted a series called Grand Rounds, where established and emerging scientists in psychology presented their current research. A fellow postdoc approached me the week before he was scheduled to present at Grand Rounds and asked if I'd be willing to take his place. He was exhausted and overworked from pulling late nights on psychiatric hospital rounds on top of his long days of clinical training, and hoped I might be able to trade spots. I was only partway through my study of Kessler's data on adolescents, and could have benefited from more time with the numbers before I shared the findings. But I was so excited by what I was learning that I leapt at the chance.

I should have been jangly with nerves as I sat in the big auditorium, waiting for the dignified and intimidating Dr. David Shaffer, chair of Columbia's Division of Child and Adolescent Psychiatry, to introduce me. A double set of metal doors slammed shut each time someone came into the room. Four of my senior colleagues strode in together and sat in the front row, rod-straight, all dressed in crisp suits. One of the women was a lead proponent of interpersonal therapy, the primary treatment model we'd used at the Children's Anxiety and Depression Clinic, where I'd met Iliana. Her landmark studies showed that what teenagers most need to learn to do is advocate for themselves, and that most teen depression stems from adolescents' inability to reconfigure their world by finding appropriate mentors and guides. The man sitting near her studied the effects of drugs on anxiety in children and adolescents. He would invite in participants, usually kids from Washington Heights—Iliana's neighborhood—and induce a panic attack. Then he would administer drugs and measure the calming effects of the medications. I respected his interest in helping young people who were suffering from anxiety. But his research methods had always struck me as unnecessarily severe. And after what I'd seen on Unit 6, I was wary of the tendency in our field to rely on medication to treat symptoms while failing to fully heal patients. But like all the faculty in the room, he was a highly credentialed, capable scientist, and this was my big chance to bring a vital finding to some of the most qualified scientists, fellow practitioners who could use it to help people.

And so, when Dr. Shaffer stepped to the podium and began

his introduction, I felt a rush of excitement. As the chair of Child and Adolescent Psychiatry, he had accepted me for the postdoc that made my work possible. A serious man in a prestigious position—a powerful leader in the Columbia University medical school, a world expert on suicide, married to the celebrated editor of *Vogue* magazine—he loved science and skipped with delight over discoveries. Today his eyes twinkled, and he ended his introduction with a personal remark.

"I never would have considered that religion or spirituality might be significant to psychiatry," he said, "until I was studying child and adolescent suicide and discovered a surprising glimmer in the data. Our rather large, school-based screening for psychopathology found that it's very difficult to identify protective factors against suicide. There was no single variable that tells us who will or won't show suicidality—except for one. Strong personal spirituality was the *only* variable inversely associated with suicide. We came upon this interesting finding quite by accident. Dr. Miller's work examines it head-on."

I practically floated up to the stage, as though lifted and carried by his support. Heart thumping, I began to share my epidemiological findings about the correlations between spirituality and lower rates of substance abuse and depression, and the numbers on the developmental and intergenerational aspects of spirituality. As I spoke and clicked through the slides, a man in the front row leaned forward, brow furrowed.

At the close of my talk, he was the first to speak. "This idea of spirituality," he said. "How did you think of it?"

Before I could utter a word, the woman sitting next to him shot up her hand and said, "I'm just trying to figure out what this data *really* means. It can't be spirituality that's making the difference."

"It's social functioning," someone else called.

"I controlled for social functioning in the analysis," I explained. "The relationship between spirituality and depression exists independent of social functioning."

"How did you measure it?" the woman in the front row asked.

I flipped back to the relevant slide. "I used the usual standardized measures," I said. "The same ones you and most faculty here use in our studies."

Many people began whispering, shuffling bags and papers, standing to leave. Those who remained squinted at me as though baffled.

"These are the standard measures for social functioning," I repeated. "There's a correlation between spirituality and mental health that is totally separate from social functioning."

My front-row colleague shook her head. "It has to be something else about social functioning," she said. "There's got to be a hidden variable underneath it all that accounts for this apparent relationship."

It was the oldest critique in the book: that some hidden variable was responsible for the finding. A hidden variable couldn't be measured or controlled for, because no one had ever found it or seen it—we didn't yet know what it was. It struck me as useful and important to cast far and wide for explanations—to leave no stone unturned. But it also seemed unscientific to discount the relevance of a clear, specific variable—in this case, spirituality—in favor of an amorphous one, one that was mere speculation, undefined and unseen. I'd walked onto the stage expecting to show a possibility for healing; it seemed I'd only succeeded in illuminating a unified discomfort.

Dr. Kendler had faced a similar critique when he published the 1997 study that had coincided with my own research trajectory. He'd been told, "What you're calling spirituality is really just personality. You didn't control for personality. You didn't look to see if this thing that looks like spirituality is just people with nonreactive temperament, or people who are introverts." He was the most distinguished genetic epidemiologist, known throughout the field for having identified the extent to which any mental illness is heritable. He had discovered that bipolar disorder is 60 percent heritable, schizophrenia more than 80 percent heritable. And everyone had accepted these findings and the scientific method he used to identify them. But the moment he touched spirituality, he had waves of critics saying, "You didn't do this carefully enough."

So in 1999, two years after the original study, he would repeat it, this time identifying the "big five" personality traits, alongside personal devotion. He'd find that the personality and spirituality traits are independent—except in one place: openness to experience. Those who are open to new experiences are also more likely to identify as spiritual. But the two don't completely overlap, and being open to new experiences doesn't necessarily cause a person to be more spiritual. His study would answer one critique raised by the original study, but it wouldn't resolve the overall discomfort around spirituality as a line of scientific inquiry.

Though we laud the so-called objectivity of science, science often follows—and ultimately reinforces—the trends of the surrounding culture. The pure method of science is objective; *how* we study a subject is rigorously defined. But *what* we study tends to shift with the tastes and appetites of the culture. At the time Dr. Kendler and I were working on the topic, in the late 1990s, there was a fascination with studying the biological foundations of psychology and mental health. No one had yet found any biological correlates of spirituality—thus spirituality didn't have a place in contemporary science or psychology. The field accepted that biology was real and that spirituality was *not* real. But this dichotomy existed only because no one had looked to see if there was a biological basis for spirituality. The accepted truth wasn't something that had actually been scientifically examined or determined. And so when my colleagues heard questions about spirituality raised in a scientific context, they couldn't figure out where it fit. They didn't see it in their models. And thus many rejected it out of hand.

After the uncomfortable reception to my presentation at Grand Rounds, I was surprised and a little nervous when Dr. Shaffer called and asked me to come to his office. I had no idea what to expect. I sat in his large corner office overlooking the Hudson River, Dr. Shaffer behind an enormous desk.

"It's quite remarkable, really, is it not?" he said.

"What?" I asked.

"Well, the *magnitude* of the finding."

I nodded. Yes, it was remarkable. That's why I'd been so eager to share the data.

"This means something extraordinary for treating young people."

I nodded again.

"I want to tell you a story," he continued. "Over the years, my wife and I have become quite close to Louanne, the administrative assistant in this department. A few years ago, Louanne's mother, who was in her nineties, fell ill with a terminal condition, and Louanne asked us to visit her. We sat in her room, having tea. Louanne's mother was propped up in bed, very ill. I asked her how she was feeling. She said, 'Oh, I'm not worried at all.' She gave me this peaceful, knowing smile and said, 'You know, my bags are packed. I'm going to meet my maker.'"

Dr. Shaffer looked at me, eyes beaming. "Isn't that something?" he said. Then he told me, "I've nominated you for a William T. Grant Faculty Scholars Award."

I also received a second, generous career development award from the National Institute of Mental Health. Both the NIMH and William T. Grant awards were prestigious and extremely respected—no one in the Columbia University Department of Psychiatry had yet to earn both. The resources attached to these awards were phenomenal: five years of funding to develop my own research in the treatment of depression, and in spiritual development and resilience in youth.

Even more thrilling was when the data I'd presented at Grand Rounds was published as another article in the orange journal, suggesting that strong science could change the field and improve how patients like Iliana were treated. To the well-meaning colleagues who had asked if questions about spirituality were pertinent to psychology, we could now definitively say, "Yes. This is risk and resilience. This is psychiatry. This is child and adolescent mental health."

CHAPTER 6

A KNOCK AT THE DOOR

Meanwhile, the relationship between biology and spirituality was playing out in my own body. Midway through my postdoc, Phil and I had decided to have a child. Parenthood had always been part of our plan, the life vision we shared as we fell in love, got married, and launched our careers. Our schooling done, careers in motion, finances steady, our fourth decade of life begun, the time was right. It wasn't so much a decision as a mutual embrace of the next logical, lovely thing.

But months passed, and I wasn't getting pregnant. Each cycle, we rode the crest of hope and then the trough of disappointment. After a number of missed attempts, my doctor ran the standard tests. Nothing concerning showed up. There was no biological reason we couldn't conceive. But more months passed, and still no baby.

"There are interventions to consider," my doctor eventually counseled. She handed me a stack of glossy, pastel-colored fertility brochures.

Phil and I pored over them that night. He still seemed content with his career change, relieved that he no longer had to don the uniform and squeeze into the crowded subway or face the dreaded elevator ride. But the commute was a problem. As long as I'd known Phil, he'd had a full, easy smile that practically loped across his face. He'd never been quick to anger. But all the honking and aggression on the highway was making him tense and irritable. He could no longer tolerate the city noise. He started sleeping on the floor in the hall of our apartment, away from the window, blankets wrapped over his head, trying to find a pocket of quiet. He'd left the job that was making him numb. But he wasn't thriving. We weren't thriving. We were both confounded by this terrain, a place we'd never been before, where neither ambition nor passion had any bearing on what came to pass. We studied the brochures and learned all the acronyms—IUI, IVF—the vocabulary itself an attempt at hope.

"What if we got out of the city?" I asked him one night. "What if we lived in the country? Do you think you'd be happy?"

"I don't know," he said. He was an East Coaster through and through, the frankest person I'd ever met—frank in a way that sometimes made people uncomfortable, though I'd always found it reassuring. I counted on him to know what he wanted and to say what he thought. "My friends are here. Who would our friends be, if we left the city?"

It was a good question. Here we had a strong network and a busy social life. And yet, we felt isolated. It was a cut-off, treadmill feeling, the perception of less even when there is more. Maybe getting out of the city would help us feel more connected to others, to each other, to ourselves. We started exploring rural New York and Connecticut on the weekends, testing it out. As we wound over country roads, watching light shift through the trees, the tension in Phil's neck and jaw would melt away. We'd stop for gas and I'd hear the chatter of birds. Even inland, when the wind turned, you could smell the sea. One Sunday I saw an OPEN HOUSE sign and made Phil pull over. Spontaneous house-hunting became part of our weekend ritual. We saw Dutch Colonials and Victorian farmhouses and architectural marvels—with ladders and catwalks and angular windows—built into the sides of cliffs. I could picture the home we were halfway looking for: a flat grassy yard, tall trees. Not suburban, but rural. Birdsong. Sheen of water.

One November day in 1997 we pulled off a twisting road in the forest a few miles inland from I-95 in Connecticut, and drove down a steep driveway. There it was. An old fishing cabin on a tiny island in the Saugatuck River. The water churned, roiling with whitecaps. It looked and sounded alive. The fast, bright water held light till late in the day, beamed it back to shore, a second sky. The longer I stood beside it, the more alive it seemed, not just the jumping water and dancing light, but the wildlife too—birds, otters—coming and going. I felt the river work over me like water on a stone—the constant rush of it, that musical sound, smoothing me out. Back in the city my thoughts were fractured and jumpy. But here, my mind didn't feel like static and particles. It was one wave. One expanse. The house itself was cozy and charming and full of light, the main part of the old cabin converted into a big open living area with giant windows along one wall, bedrooms tacked onto each side. I knew it right away: this was a place we could raise a family.

It wasn't until we'd bought the house and stood in the living room in late winter, exhausted, surrounded by heaps of boxes and belongings, that Phil looked at me in panic. "Where are we going to go out for Chinese food?"

There wasn't a scrap of food in the house, and of course no restaurant or bodega or falafel stand around the corner. There was no corner. Just our lip of quiet land and the tiny bridge to the other shore. We piled into the car. In all our trips out here, we hadn't paid attention to the town centers and strip malls. They didn't interest us. We'd been so busy scouting the ideal life, we hadn't made a plan for our actual life. We thought we could turn a switch and become country people. But we didn't know how to survive out here. Where were we going to eat?

Phil drove too fast on the curves toward town. It was almost eight o'clock. Would anything be open? We screeched onto Post Road, the main street in Westport, a stretch of low-slung strip malls. Most of the windows were dark. Dry-cleaner. Pharmacy. All closed. But then we saw it—a neon flicker, the only sign still lit, our beacon. Phil whipped into the near-empty parking lot and we raced inside Angelina's Trattoria just as the manager was about to lock up. Seeing our hopeful faces, he ushered us in and we collapsed into the vinyl chairs and ordered pizza. Phil shook his head forlornly, pointing out the window to a sign in the dark parking lot. POST PLAZA, it said, but the P was damaged, pieces of the letter broken off and hanging.

"We're at the Lost Plaza," he said.

We drove home, brightly lit houses shining through the trees. We could glimpse the families inside, someone at a kitchen sink, cozy groups of parents and children clustered by a fire or in front of a TV. But when we pulled down the driveway to our new home, all was dark. We were still so far from the life we wanted.

A FEW MONTHS LATER, in the spring of 1998, after another cycle without conceiving, Phil and I stood at the bathroom sink one night, brushing our teeth. He turned to me.

"We could give IUI a try," he said.

Artificial insemination was the least invasive of the available procedures. We went through the procedure twice. Still no baby. On the third attempt, a new nurse was at the clinic, a temporary substitute. She was about forty-five years old. She hummed as she adjusted me on the table and prepped the syringe.

"All right!" she said, releasing Phil's cells inside me. "A life is beginning."

And just like that, for the first time, we conceived. Even in those early, early weeks, the joy of carrying a life within permeated my sense of self. Phil and I were going to be parents! I was holding a tiny light inside me and felt its warmth and hope and promise. In mere months we would meet a completely unique little human whom we already loved to the core. Even the mundane moments of life—doing the dishes, clearing mail off the kitchen table, driving to my office at Columbia—felt inherently meaningful because of the consuming, abiding love for our child.

The night before my first ultrasound, I dreamt I was in my childhood home in St. Louis, in the pink-flowered kitchen where I'd spent so much time with my mother, this place of nourishment and life, where I'd been taken care of so well. In the dream I stand at the sink, in my mother's place. Suddenly, the deepest grief hits me. I fall to the floor on my knees, crying, "He's dead, and I never got to know him."

I woke with relief. It was only a dream. A nightmare. Sad and haunting, but not true. I stroked my belly. I didn't mention the dream to Phil. To name it would give it too much credit. *I'm pregnant!* I told myself over and over as I showered and dressed. Whatever dregs of the dream still cluttered my head, I dismissed, I shook away. *I'm pregnant!* By the time I was on my way to the clinic for the ultrasound, I'd overturned the sorrow of the dream. Wiped it clean.

When the ultrasound technician passed the wand over my

abdomen, the cold gel tickled. I was giddy in anticipation of the first glimpse of our child, and I closed my eyes in the darkened room, feeling the glide of the wand over my skin.

Then the wand stopped. "I'll get the doctor," the technician said.

My bare belly felt cold. Goosebumps rose on my arms as I waited for the doctor. She came in briskly, made a few passes with the wand, and said matter-of-factly, "The baby's heart is stopped."

Suddenly the light had gone out. My doctor could find no medical reason why my body had not sustained the pregnancy. But the loss was acute. Life had been; now it wasn't.

I had to go home and tell Phil. He curled into a little ball when I spoke the words. I held him as he convulsed with tears. I'd never seen him cry like that.

My friends, many of whom were pregnant or parenting infants, were encouraging. "When you've been pregnant once," they said, "it's so much easier to get pregnant again."

But it didn't happen. Phil and I remained fixated on our desire for a baby. Yet the thing we wanted so badly just didn't come. We sought fertility experts all over Manhattan and then went doggedly up and down the East Coast, determined to find the right doctor or clinic. I called women I'd gone to high school with who'd had successful in vitro fertility treatments. If their doctor was in Boston, I went to Boston.

We stayed in Boston with my parents one weekend so that I could make an early-morning appointment and still be home to teach that afternoon. I went into the study to get something out of the closet, and discovered that it was full of baby clothes. Little outfits in blue and pink and yellow, arranged in ascending order from infant sizes up to one year. My mom had apparently started shopping for her grandchild as soon as I'd shared the happy news that I was pregnant. That full closet, all that tucked-away hope, the anticipation of a sacred little person who wasn't yet to be. It tore me up.

Even worse were those agonizing minutes in the chair after we'd made another attempt, the gel-topped wand passing over my belly, waiting, waiting to hear a heartbeat. That became our state of being. Waiting for something that never came.

I'd walk along the quaint streets in small-town Connecticut and see people pushing baby carriages, holding toddlers' hands. I'd go to my friends' baby showers and try not to flinch as the ornate little outfits were lifted out of the tissue paper–lined boxes. We kept trying fertility treatments. They kept failing. I'd go straight to my planner and schedule another appointment. But I wasn't getting pregnant. And the deeper my craving to have a child, the more depressed and empty I felt each time we were disappointed. I knew I was stuck. But I didn't know how to switch modes.

And so, in early 2000, Phil and I were sitting in yet another IVF clinic—this time, the fertility clinic at the University of Pennsylvania in Philadelphia, home of the scientists who had researched sea urchins at Woods Hole and invented in vitro fertility treatment.

"Of course we can get you pregnant," the doctor said.

I'd lost count of the times a respected practitioner at a top-notch facility had said these exact words. I tried to ignore the feeling in my gut that he was wrong, that every time I went to an IVF clinic hoping to become a mother, I was knocking on the wrong door. It wasn't just my intuition telling me to stop. It was my body, too. I'd had so many injections that my stomach was swollen with bruises, and I was concerned that all the hormones would make me sick.

And yet, there was no physiological reason anyone could find that explained why I wasn't getting pregnant, and so I told myself not to lose hope. *This doctor has a great success rate,* my brain insisted. I signed the forms and waivers, I took the drugs, and the doctor implanted an embryo in my womb.

I had to be on bed rest, and Phil stayed in the hotel room with me in solidarity. We were at a beautiful place in Rittenhouse Square, in a room that looked out on a peaceful park. We cozied up, ordered food, and looked for something good on TV. But when Phil tried to flip through the channels, the remote wouldn't work. We were stuck on a channel showing a depressing documentary shot in a garbage dump in Rio de Janeiro. A little boy, an orphan, stood on a heap of trash, interviewed through a translator.

"I don't care that I can't go to school," he said. "I don't care that I live in the garbage dump. But it hurts so much *to not be loved* that I sniff glue to make the pain go away."

I caught my breath. I looked at Phil.

He said it first: "There's a child out there for us."

I DIDN'T KNOW what seeing the orphan on TV meant, or if anything outward would change in our quest to become parents. I still desperately wanted to get pregnant. I still struggled with uncertainty and discouragement. But it also felt significant to have heard the orphan's story at that time. It gave me a flicker of hope, recognition that the boy and I were part of the same reality, the same whole.

When the IVF treatment failed again, the familiar despair closed in. But a new feeling threaded through the dark—a sense of curiosity about how things might unfold.

· · ·

ONE AFTERNOON LATER that year, I came home from yet another IVF treatment, heavy with the familiar feeling that it
wouldn't work. As I neared the front door, head foggy and out
of sorts, I happened to glance down and see something on the
doorstep: black, wet, the size of a finger. I stooped to examine it.
A beak and tiny webbed feet dangled askew. It was a duck embryo. I used a piece of mail to scoot it gently onto the earth
beside the door.

I got into bed with my clothes on and took a long, depressing nap. I dreaded Phil's return home and the next OB appointment when yet again we'd likely learn that the embryo had not
implanted—that it had failed to find its home. I finally woke to
a persistent tapping, loud and clear over the racing river. When I
peered out the front window, I saw a full-grown duck, a female,
thrusting her beak at the door. *Tap, tap, tap.* I opened the door
and found that the mama duck had brought me a gift: a plump,
juicy worm. She dropped it on the threshold and waddled back
toward the river.

In that moment, my inner life and outer life lined up in a way
that felt significant, too improbable to have happened by chance.
I felt guided by something, a larger order or life force. In that
moment, I saw the mama duck as evidence of the deep connection possible between living beings, a feeling of oneness. Even
hope.

CHAPTER 7

WHEN INNER AND OUTER ALIGN

After the first duck-knock on the door, more synchronistic moments arose. I was on a bus in New York and, out of the blue, a stranger next to me said, "You seem like the type of mother who would go all around the world, adopting all kinds of kids."

A few days later, my mom called. She's a frequent volunteer in my parents' suburban Boston community, and she had been working on a project with someone who hadn't been pulling her weight.

"Normally, I wouldn't say anything," she told me. "I'd just keep doing my part. But I was doing ninety percent, and it was too much, and I was about to confront her. But then she tells me she's preoccupied because she's just adopted a baby from Russia. She invited me over to meet him. Robert Abraham. Her beautiful little boy, as healthy as can be. Such a darling."

Synchronicity was building on synchronicity. It was as though perceiving synchronicity once, with the orphan on TV, and then again with the mama duck, had opened the way to perceiving more and more synchronicities. I had the sensation that, just as in an archetypal quest, I was becoming open, ever so gradually, to the guidance of helpers and healers on my journey. I was becoming aware of what hikers on the Pacific Crest and Appalachian trails call "trail angels"—the people who offer food and help and respite to weary hikers. I still had a long journey ahead, full of unknowns. But I didn't feel anymore that I was alone. I could sense that I was being held with support and caring by others along the path.

But there was nothing in psychology that accounted for what I was experiencing personally and clinically. There was no model that adequately described or explained the lift and ease I felt when my inner and outer life synced up—a buoyancy that came not from getting what I wanted, but from suddenly seeing my place in the world anew. Psychology held what seemed too limited a view on healing: that we scan the world and knit together meaning; that we feel better when we are able to choose to make a brighter meaning from the stuff in our lives. What I was witnessing in my fertility journey and in treating patients was less that we heal when we *impose* a more positive meaning on the world, and more that we shift toward health when somehow, and usually through struggle, a bigger meaning is *revealed* to us. Synchronicity seemed to be one way, even in darkness and suffering, for a new sense of the world to show up or shine through.

Now a professor at Teachers College, Columbia University, I had created a graduate-level course in spirituality and psychology—the first offering of its kind at any Ivy League institution. The first time I taught the class, I gave students an assignment toward the beginning of the semester to write about a time they trusted their deep inner knowing and understood intuitively that something had meaning, even if no one else had pointed them toward that understanding, or if others disagreed. Each week, the students came to class empty-handed. "Could you give us more clarity on that exercise?" they'd say. "We're not quite sure what you want. What do you mean by 'knowing'?" Each week, I'd repeat the instructions: "I want you to tell about a time when you knew something to be true even though others might have told you that you were wrong or mistaken."

Finally, after five or six weeks of going around and around like this, a young woman with dark curly hair raised her hand. "It's interesting," she said. "Dr. Miller, you explain this assignment very clearly, and then we come back the next week full of questions and ask you to explain again. I think it's because we've spent all these years from kindergarten through college, and now graduate school, trying to figure out what the teacher or professor wants, and trying to learn the ideas we're supposed to understand. And after so much time worrying about what we're supposed to think, we don't know what we think." She pointed to the irony of becoming more and more educated while becoming less and less able to trust ourselves as knowers.

What happens when we learn—or relearn—how to validate our perceptions as real? To trust ourselves to know in many forms? Synchronicity—when two apparently disparate events are joined at the level of meaning or consciousness—seemed like an accessible way to illuminate and validate those sparks of inner knowing, those flashes of meaning or insight that seem to arrive out of the blue.

Jung talked about three different kinds of synchronicity: (1) when events in your inner and outer life are linked expressions of the same event (such as when I dreamt about losing the baby and miscarried the next day); (2) when two or more events in your outer life are linked expressions of the same event (the man on the bus and my mom talking to me about international adoption); and (3) when events experienced by different people are linked expressions of the same event (the orphan on TV talking about his desire to be loved at the same time that Phil and I were searching for a child to love). In a purely mechanistic understanding of life, there's no way that two separate events can be part of the same unified whole. The events are either unrelated or linked by direct cause and effect. But Jung suggested two things: first, that two mechanistically separate events are actually one at the level of consciousness; and second, that there is no real difference between inner and outer life.

My graduate students and I began to explore synchronicity as an element of spiritual awakening. One student—Lydia Cho, who went on to become a psychologist and neuropsychologist at Harvard Medical School's McLean Hospital—developed a study on synchronicity. She conducted and analyzed semi-structured interviews at the start and end of a workshop, calling attention to the experience, and found that the more aware of synchronicity participants became, the more synchronicity they experienced. The more we pay attention to synchronicity, the more it becomes apparent, as though when our eyes are more open to it, synchronicity picks up steam, growing more forthcoming and abundant.

Cho also found that this enhanced perception of synchronicity goes hand in hand with increased spiritual awareness—and with better mental health. The more we practice engaging with open awareness, the more we are able to perceive synchronicity. And as we see synchronicity, we become more spiritually oriented—more aware of guidance, connection, and unity in our lives.

I wanted to know the why of it, and how.

. . .

DR. MARC BERMAN and his colleagues at the University of Chicago have since done a number of studies on attention, and have shown that when we focus on an a priori goal or idea and look out into the environment, we're scanning on behalf of that idea. And when we engage this top-down perception, it filters what we see. On the one hand, this is helpful. The goal or idea helps narrow our focus to perceive the things that are relevant to it. But the idea or goal also limits our perceptual field. Our brains fail to perceive anything that doesn't fit with the a priori idea. For example, if you wake up in the morning with the idea of going for a drive, when you look around the room you're already scanning for your keys and sunglasses, wondering if you should make coffee before you leave or buy some on the road. You engage your top-down attention, narrowing your observations and thoughts to serve your goal of getting on the road. This is a helpful way of looking at the world. It allows us to take action—to get out the door without getting distracted by news headlines or unwashed dishes or any number of things that might snag our attention. Top-down attention helps us stay focused on the task or idea or goal at hand.

But top-down perception isn't the only way to look at the world. And it's not always the best way. Sometimes we're better served by engaging bottom-up perception. It's a more open and present way of seeing what's there; you're not just scanning the room and selectively attending to whatever serves your goal. Therefore, you have a wider perceptual range. And what is most salient or emotionally relevant pops out at you. For instance, at a time when you've been feeling misgivings about your poor communication with your brother, you pass teen siblings on the sidewalk, and they remind you of your own sibling relationship back when you were growing up. Or after navigating a tide of toddler meltdowns, a mother singing to her baby in a grocery cart suddenly reminds you of the joy of being a parent. What you see might break the cycle of familiar thoughts and concerns stirring around in your head, or wake you up to a blind spot. The new observation strikes you as emotionally rich or significant, and shows you a new direction, perhaps prompting you to gain new insights or actions. The Berman and related studies open the door to the notion that through learning to engage our bottom-up attention we might build up the muscle of perception that, as Cho's work suggests, better allows us to see synchronicity.

Synchronicity isn't just a matter of perception or awareness. It's also a physical phenomenon—something that actually happens in the world. At a moment of personal loss, I really had found a duck embryo on my doorstep, and I'd found it on that particular day, not weeks or months or years in the past or future. A mama duck really had brought a worm to the door. A stranger on a bus who couldn't possibly know anything of my struggle had mentioned international adoption. Many of us have these experiences. We might suddenly think of someone we haven't seen or spoken to or even thought of in ages, and the next day we bump into him on a crowded street. Or we might pick up the phone to call or text a friend at the same instant that she's calling or texting us, without any external reason that can explain the coincidence.

It makes sense that if we engage bottom-up perception, we're more likely to notice synchronistic events. But what *causes* synchronicity to occur in the first place? What makes our inner and outer realities align in what seems like random, improbable coincidence?

.   .   .

SINCE ISAAC NEWTON published the foundations of classical physics in the late 1600s, we've understood that there are mathematical equations that govern and explain foundational properties of the physical world. We can predict what will happen when we throw a ball or turn a crank or otherwise act upon the world. We have useful, accurate, consistent information about the way the physical world behaves. For example, Newton's innovative understanding of gravity and the laws of motion, though revolutionary at the time, are now unshakable, foundational ways of understanding how the world works.

But as physicists discovered more than one hundred years ago, classical Newtonian physics doesn't always work. It works for everyday objects moving at everyday speeds. But it doesn't work when we try to predict or describe the behavior of very small things (electrons and particles), very big things (stars), or very complex things (living systems). A new branch of physics— quantum physics—emerged from the inability of classical physics to accurately describe all of reality. Quantum theory explains the surprising behaviors of electrons and particles—the things we didn't know about fundamental aspects of our world until we started asking questions about the physical world at a smaller and smaller and larger and larger scale. Quantum physics has enabled major technological advances like computers, digital cameras, lasers, and LEDs. And it may help explain the physical properties of synchronicity.

One of the first scientists to illuminate a vital aspect of quantum physics was British physicist Thomas Young. Though he worked strictly within the classical physics paradigm, his double-slit experiment in 1801 revealed what has turned out to be one of the major principles of quantum physics—that matter can actually behave like waves, and vice versa. At that time, it was largely agreed that light was made of particles. But when Young shone a light source at a metal plate that was pierced by two narrow parallel slits, and put a screen behind the plate so he could observe what happened as the light passed through the slits, he saw something surprising. The light didn't hit the screen in two discrete patches that matched the size and shape of the two slits, as expected. The light passing through the slits actually formed an alternating pattern of light and dark bands across the screen. Young concluded that the bands were caused by an interference pattern formed when two waves of light passed simultaneously through the slits. The bright bands were places where the waves added to each other; the dark bands were places where the waves canceled each other out. This banded interference pattern was only possible if light is made up of waves, not particles.

But it turns out it isn't that simple. Light doesn't behave like particles *or* waves. It behaves like both. Later double-slit experiments showed that individual light photons could be detected passing independently through each slit, and that light was absorbed by the screen at discrete points, as though the screen was being hit by individual particles, not washed by a wave. Even more surprising, in the early 1900s, scientists performed double-slit experiments using electrons—tiny bits of matter—and found that they exhibit the same wave-particle duality. Now we know this is also true of atoms and molecules. All physical things behave like waves *and* particles.

But how can this be? Particles and waves seem contradictory by nature. Particles are localized, their position measurable in space and time. A particle is like a tiny tennis ball—even in motion, it can only be in one exact place at a time, and it always moves along a predictable, measurable trajectory. Waves, on the other hand, aren't localized. They constantly disperse and spread out; they exist in more than one place at a time. Their frequency can be measured, but they don't have a precise location.

Quantum theory resolves this paradox by asserting that waves underlie all of reality—that at a fundamental level, everything behaves like waves of energy and "chance." Before particles are particles with an exact position or energy or speed, they are waves—existing across all possible states at the same time. Before particles become particles, they exist as quantum waves, represented by abstract mathematical wave functions that show all the possible measurements we might make on the object (position, energy, speed, etc.), and the probability that you'll get a particular result when you make the measurement—that you'll find the object at a particular location *if you look*. How does a quantum wave become a localized particle? We don't know. But we could also say that when a wave function collapses into a particle with a precise location, the only thing that has changed is our measuring it—in other words, our paying attention. It is precisely our act of measuring that makes the wave measurable—that gives it a specific, localized presence. Something that exists in quantum reality begins to exist in everyday reality *through our observation* of it. Our attention collapses the wave of possibility into a single point.

German physicist Werner Heisenberg had another way of describing how our attention, as an intervention, changes reality. According to the Heisenberg uncertainty principle, it's impossible to precisely measure the position *and* momentum of a particle at the same time. This is because you can't make an observation without perturbing the system you're measuring. If you accurately measure the position of a particle, you necessarily disturb its momentum. Because of the inherent wave quality of all objects, *indeterminacy* is built into the fabric of reality. To measure one aspect of reality with certainty sends other aspects into flux. To know one thing means to un-know something else. Two seemingly separate things are actually related; they're expressions of one whole.

Along with wave-particle duality and the uncertainty principle, a third quantum property—quantum entanglement—completely revolutionized the classical Newtonian take on reality. Albert Einstein and his colleagues Boris Podolsky and Nathan Rosen first discussed entanglement in a theoretical way in 1935; beginning in 1964, scientists John Bell and Alain Aspect and others showed entanglement in an experimental, not just theoretical, way. Entanglement happens when particles become so intimately correlated that what occurs for one co-occurs for the other, even across vast distances—as far as light-years apart.

For example, if a pair of electrons is created together, one will have a spin in an upward direction, and the other will have a downward spin. But neither particle has a definite spin until it is measured. They're in superposition: their spins are simultaneously linked *and* unknown. Another way to think about it is that until their spins are measured, both electrons are simultaneously spin-up *and* spin-down. But when they're separated and measured, each has a definite, known spin. And one will always be measured spin-up and the other will always be measured spin-down. So how does a possible spin become a definite spin? And how does each electron "know" to have a spin that correlates with its partner electron?

Einstein was so flummoxed by entanglement that he called it "spooky action at a distance" and maintained throughout his life that some hidden variable must account for the seemingly instantaneous communication between electrons that are too far apart to influence one another by classically accepted means. But Einstein was grappling with a common assumption so reasonable that it didn't even seem like an assumption. People at that time assumed a reality bounded by locality—that everything about a particle is fixed in one location. But, quantum physics asks, what if we don't assume locality? What if particles, even when separated at a distance, are connected? What if particles can exist in more than one place *at the same time*?

For three hundred years, physics was predicated on the notion that objects that are far apart can't directly influence one another. This became our accepted understanding of the way the world is built. Quantum theory resolves the seeming paradox of entanglement with nonlocality—the understanding that properties of entangled particles are correlated even when it would seem impossible for the particles to influence or affect one another. Numerous experiments since 1964 have shown that the effects of nonlocality are real. Quantum physics says we can no longer think of two particles as separate entities; somehow, they are part of the same entity. The world isn't made of individual particles. It's an inseparable whole. And our attention is what beholds both expressions of reality: point and wave, distinctness and oneness.

Could quantum physics offer an explanation or guidepost for how and why synchronicity occurs? If particles are entangled—interconnected and correlated across vast distances—might humans, made up of many particles, be intimately and inextricably entangled, too? And might synchronistic experiences be those moments when a wave of possibility is discernible as a particle? When someone else's "spin-up" determines our "spin-down"?

And could quantum physics provide a new paradigm for psychology? A way to perceive and navigate a reality in which we are both particles *and* waves?

Marty Seligman once told me about a symposium at the University of Pennsylvania where a speaker played music and turned on blinking Christmas lights and asked the audience to detect the relationship between the patterns of sound and light. People put forward various theories, different ratios to describe the relationship between the beat of the music and the on-and-off of the lights. Then, after people had passionately argued their theories, the speaker revealed that actually, there was no pattern—that the sound and lights weren't at all connected. That to detect a relationship was to impose a unifying meaning onto random, disconnected parts. That meaning is imputed, not inherent.

It seemed that this was the place where psychology had become stuck, in a view of reality as incomplete as Newton's, bound by three limiting assumptions: (1) that the brain creates thoughts; (2) that all meaning is interpretation; and (3) that we can feel better by rearranging our thoughts—by disputing the thoughts that make us unhappy, and replacing depressing thoughts with a new framework that helps us tell a brighter story. But what if the brain didn't create thoughts so much as receive them? What if our brains were less like idea generators and more like antennae or docking stations for a larger consciousness? What if to feel better is actually to detect and be in alignment with that consciousness? What if emotions direct us into the world as it really is?

What I was discovering about synchronicity suggested something important about healing: that feeling better isn't just a matter of creating new thoughts, of replacing unhappy ones with happier ones—it's also about noticing and aligning ourselves with whatever life is showing us. This doesn't mean we get crisp or obvious answers to a priori questions. Life isn't a mail-order catalog. We don't send our attention out, and then get the goods or the answer we ordered. Spiritual awareness is a stance, not a transaction. There's never a guarantee that we're going to get what we want, or what we thought we wanted. When we become spiritually aware—through synchronicity, for example—

it's a sign that despite the uncertainty, we are aligned with the force of life.

When I saw the duck embryo and received the worm, I didn't get pregnant the next month. Nor did I discard my desire to be a mom and decide that my life would be better without kids. I woke from a depressing nap and was granted a sudden glimpse that I'm part of a deep interconnectedness. That I'm being buoyed up, that I'm in the right place, I'm on my path, I'm part of the field of life. I was suffering, wondering if I could go on without a child. And then I heard life essentially telling me, *There's so much love and relationship and interconnectedness all around us. You are part of the oneness of life.* Depression wasn't the thing that had obscured my view of the bigger picture. It was the knock on the door.

LATER IN 2000, a few months after finding the duck embryo, I sat with Phil in a small room of a Pittsburgh adoption agency, every wall plastered with photos of smiling families from all over the United States who'd adopted babies and children from Russia. After the most recent unsuccessful attempt at IVF, Phil and I had turned back to the impulse that had arisen in the hotel room in Philadelphia as we watched the documentary of the boy at the garbage dump who had longed for love. There were children all over the world longing for love—and we were longing to give it. My mom had put us in touch with the agency that had sponsored her friend's adoption of Robert Abraham. They'd insisted we could fill out the initial paperwork and questionnaires from home, but once we'd decided to look into the possibility of adopting, I needed to make eye contact with the people who might help match us with a child.

"You need to tell me honestly," the woman from the agency

said. "What do you want in a child?" Sophie Gurel leaned right up to me with a frank, piercing gaze. She was sixty years old, the daughter of a rabbi, and took finding a match of parent and child extremely seriously.

I looked around us at all the happy families. There were infants swaddled in cotton blankets, toddlers in strollers and wagons, older kids who'd lost their front teeth, teenagers wearing graduation gowns and waving diplomas. The one element evident in every single photograph was love. It struck me: the definition of parenting is love; to be a parent means to love in a new capacity. I'd been so caught up in the goal of finally having a child—or, really, just getting pregnant—that I had lost sight of the larger view: to be a parent is to live the greatest love story.

"I don't care what race this child is," I said. "I don't care about gender. But please, I want a child who *can love*."

She looked at Phil. "What about you?"

"Everything that Lisa said is true for me. But . . ." He grinned sheepishly. "But I'd kind of like a girl."

That night, Pittsburgh's professional ice hockey team won a playoff game and the town erupted—music blasting, parties in the street. We took a walk, riding that energy and ebullience. For the first time since my initial pregnancy years earlier, I felt like I was on the right trajectory.

To parent is to love. I knew it intellectually. I knew it from the way my parents loved me—the warmth around our table, my mom's bright eyes and tinkling laugh when she asked about my day, my dad's steady thoughtfulness, the way he would slowly nod his head as he considered something I had said. But sitting in the Pittsburgh adoption agency that day, surrounded by images of exquisitely loving families, it struck me in a new way. Love is the foundation of it all. I sensed that love would be essential to my journey toward motherhood.

. . .

A FEW NIGHTS LATER, I had a profound experience. I suddenly woke out of a deep sleep. Phil was breathing softly beside me. I sensed a sort of charged brightness in the room, though no lights were shining in. And I felt something I can only describe as a presence there with us. My heart started racing. I sat straight up in bed. The presence spoke to me. I didn't hear it exactly. I sensed it, felt its resonance. *If you were pregnant, would you adopt?* the powerful presence asked.

"No," I said into the night. My answer had come right out of my mouth before I could consider the question. But I knew it was the truth. I wanted a baby in my body, an expression of Phil's and my love, a being to carry on all we had received from our families, who looked like us. I wanted it above all else.

As soon as I spoke, the presence was gone. The space it had occupied, whoever or whatever had visited me, closed again, and then the darkness folded back.

CHAPTER 8

CALLING ALL LOST SONS

Hey, Miss Columbia Professor," my cousin Jane teased in the spring of 2001. "I thought you were supposed to be the smart one!"

I was standing at the check-in gate in the Iowa airport, the gate agents' phone pressed to my ear, disoriented from my last-minute flight to Sioux City. When I stepped off the plane onto the rickety metal stairs, I'd been overcome by the scent of the fertile prairie. This far from the ocean, you could smell the earth—rich, sweet, and deeply familiar, though I hadn't been back to the Midwest in years.

The unexpected trip was a last-ditch effort on my quest to become a mother. Jane had called me at home and said in her frank, down-to-earth way, "If you're still trying for a child—and if you really want to understand what's going on—you need to come out here. Tomorrow." A clinical social worker and therapist, she sometimes worked with a nearby community of Lakota healers who would be gathering for a daylong ceremony. Thinking they might be able to guide me in ways that Western medical science hadn't, she'd requested and received permission for me to attend with her. I put a hand on my belly, the patchwork of welts and bruises from the constant injections. I could no longer count the number of failed IVF treatments, and I didn't think Phil or I could endure the constant cycle of loss any longer. Was I open to a different kind of intervention, something far outside my training as a scientist? I took the phone outside and stood barefoot on the deck, watching the river tumble over the rocks, evening light caught up in the tumult. "I'll come," I said.

But the journey was off to an inauspicious start.

"You're in the wrong Sioux," Jane said through the airport phone.

I was supposed to be in Sioux Falls, South Dakota—but I'd flown to Sioux City, Iowa, almost a hundred miles away.

"Classic rookie mistake," Jane said. "If you start driving now, you'll still be in time for supper."

Jane, whom I'd always called Big Jane, was thirteen years older than me, as close to my parents in age as she was to me. With half a generation between us, she had been more of a mentor and advocate than a peer. In one of my earliest baby pictures, taken in 1967, she lies beside me, dressed in a yellow-and-gray plaid miniskirt, gazing into my eyes as though I'm *her* baby. She'd always been fiercely protective of me, and also determined that I hear the truth about everything, that reality never be sugar-coated. She told me the real scoop on family disputes, gave me *Our Bodies, Ourselves* before I hit puberty, and, though she relished in my successes, had a way of bringing me down to earth.

I rented a car and drove out into the spring sunshine, headed due north, across the open plains, feeling displaced and also deeply reassured by the markers of my long-ago home—the startling green of the trees at that time of year, the way people talked, that familiar economy of midwestern vowels. I'd forgotten how vast and planar the Iowa fields are. Mounds of tilled earth, vibrant green shoots emerging, soon to grow into towering stalks of corn. Endless rows and furrows that spread as far as I could see on either side of the interstate, broken only by red barns and white farmhouses with wide, inviting front porches.

I flipped the radio dial, catching strains of country music—that strange mix of hope and mournfulness—conservative talk radio, Christian music. The upbeat religious songs reminded me of early, early mornings in St. Louis when I was a girl. Despite my Jewish upbringing, I would get up on Sundays long before my parents, even before the bars on the television had transitioned to programming, so I wouldn't miss a single minute of the gospel choirs that performed one after another through the morning. I'd forgotten those soulful Mississippi River singers in their long robes, how joyful I'd felt as a child as I jumped around in my nightgown, dancing with each group in turn. That unbridled joy felt foreign now. I'd been immersed for so long in the rigors and rituals of academic life and scientific research, troubled by infertility. But now, far from my current home and familiar routines, it struck me: what I'd been doing was all wrong. As my cousin Jane had joked on the phone, smart alone wasn't solving this.

The western horizon was turning amber and rose as I reached Sioux Falls, the fields flaming gold. I suddenly felt vulnerable under all that open sky. Exposed. Alone. A wave of worry and doubt rippled through me.

Was I just opening the door to another dead end? I knew next to nothing about the people I'd been invited to meet or what we'd be doing together, what the spiritual process would entail. I'd always had an intellectual interest in Native American cultures, and I included some Native American spiritual texts on the syllabus for my course on spirituality and psychology. But I hadn't come to South Dakota for an academic exercise, or an anthropological study. Big Jane had invited me to encounter a way of being and healing that was completely foreign to me. Was I really open to it? How would it square with my scientific training and empirical understanding of the world?

I think we all get a call of some kind at various points in our lives. Maybe not a literal phone call, but a sort of suggestion or prompting that forces us to consider how far we're willing to go to change things, or find the truth, or discover what we're missing. Big Jane's invitation felt like this kind of lifeline, and on the prairie at sunset, something shifted inside me. I still felt sad and hollow. But I also sensed that I was on the threshold of something new, at the tip of another point of view. I pulled off the highway and drove toward the setting sun, guided by the one thing I always hold, even throughout pervasive doubt and confusion: my certainty as a scientist that anything true can be shown.

WHEN I REACHED Big Jane's house in Vermillion, South Dakota, she folded me into a warm hug and led me into the kitchen, which smelled like beets freshly pulled from the earth, dirt on the skins, plumes of greens still attached. She was the first person I knew who'd become a vegan, long before it was a mainstream option. Her frank, hands-on sensibility permeated the house—organic, unprocessed foods, handmade quilts, spare wood lines. She pulled a steaming vegetable casserole from the oven and pointed me to a stack of woven placemats and earth-tone ceramic dishes to arrange on the dark wood table. Jane had always had a knack for meeting people's distress with enormous courage and a complete lack of judgment. As she rinsed rich green leaves of spinach and romaine and chopped carrots and tomatoes for the salad, she prepped me for the next day.

The healing ritual would be broken into two parts. In the morning, the whole community of participants would gather in the Rotary Club lodge to share personal stories—the situations and circumstances for which they sought healing. No one was required to speak; all were invited. In the evening, men and women would separate for the *inipi,* a purification and prayer ritual. We'd enter a sweat lodge, a temporary structure built for the ceremony, and the healer would draw on the sacred power of earth, water, fire, and air to offer prayers for healing.

"The ritual is all about spiritual rebirth," she said, tossing the salad with big wooden spoons. *Inipi* means "to live again," and the *inipi* structure represents the womb of the universe from which we'd emerge cleansed and reborn.

I put my hands on my belly—the universal motion of pregnant women already loving and protecting life within. For me it was a reflexive gesture forever coupled with the ache of loss. Tears welled in my eyes. Jane passed me on her way to the table with the salad bowl and brushed her hand across my back.

Her husband and two daughters—Michaela in middle school, Eva in high school—joined us at the table. I hadn't seen them since they were in preschool. Now they were confident, capable young women, as realistic and forthright as their mother, chatting about their classes and friends. My beloved, down-to-earth cousin had created a family. I ate with a lump in my throat.

WHEN I WALKED into the Rotary Club lodge the next morning for the first part of the healing ritual, I had the awkward, displaced feeling of being at a stranger's family reunion. I stuck out like a sore thumb. Jane and I were some of the only white people in attendance. About two hundred folding chairs were lined up in the room, and I sat toward the back, where I could try to blend in and be a respectful observer.

No one had to announce the organization of the day—the structure seemed to be clear to everyone. Things flowed as though spontaneously. One by one, people came up to the microphone at the front of the room to tell their stories. They spoke as long as they desired, many sharing the pain and challenges of PTSD or addiction or sexual abuse, some speaking as long as twenty minutes, everyone listening with complete and unbroken focus. As each person finished sharing, the drums would start. Everyone rose with the drums, lining up single file to talk privately with the speaker, sharing that which had moved their heart. Some whispered, some leaned in as they spoke. Each member of the community showed up in this way for every single speaker, as though they were part of a web in which every strand was connected.

Speaking is my day job. I can speak in front of a class, at a professional conference, never nervous or tongue-tied when addressing a crowd. But I couldn't speak there in the lodge. I knew I was an invited guest; I felt welcome to be there and participate, and Jane, my fierce and loving advocate, was beside me. But I couldn't bring myself to speak. I knew how to research fertility clinics and schedule treatments. I didn't know how to tell my story, to ask for help in a deeper way. So I listened.

At one point a chief stood up, tears in his eyes. He opened his arms. "My son," he said, "who I adopted first in my heart, we are bound together by Wakan Tanka, the Great Spirit, bound in all dimensions." A chill went down my spine. My mind flashed on the photos of loving families on the walls of the adoption agency in Pittsburgh.

For eight hours, people listened and shared and responded.

No one stepped outside. After an evening break to eat and re-fresh, we returned for the second half of the ritual. We entered the *inipi* at nightfall.

When I stepped into the domed tent made from willow trees and draped with animal hides, I felt even more awkward and displaced than I had in the lodge. A fire burned inside, the heat intense, the tent full of smoke. We sat in a circle on a bed of sage. Jane and I were the only non-Lakota women there. Everyone else wore jeans and blouses or shirts. I was dressed like I was going to brunch, in black pumps and a skirt with white polka dots. The heat was almost unbearable. Near the base of the tent was a small crack where a tiny wisp of cold fresh air came in, and I tried to inch myself closer to the gap.

My blouse was already drenched in sweat by the time the medicine woman opened the ceremony. She began a prayer, looking at each of us in turn. When her eyes rested on me, she wove a welcome into her prayer to the Great Spirit: "I do not know who this woman is and I do not know why she has come, but you have sent her," she intoned. "So let me help her."

The heat flared. Each woman was invited to speak in turn, to say why she had come, to share her suffering and need for heal-ing. One woman spoke of her son. He was in his forties, grap-pling with addiction. He had stopped coming home. Another woman's son, a boy of fourteen, had started using drugs. So many women shared about their sons—sons who were sick or hurt or disappearing. The sharing moved in a circle. I was the very last. Big Jane was on my left. When the circle of sharing reached Jane, I could feel her understand that still I had no words. She spoke for me.

"I am Big Jane, and this is my cousin Lisa Jane," she said. "She has come searching for her child. Can we help her find her child?"

The women in the dark around the fire looked at me with deep attention. They nodded, they *mmm'd*. Their presence felt solid around me, sustaining. Here, the need for healing was not synonymous with brokenness. It was part of life. And these women understood the experience of looking for your child.

The medicine woman recited a prayer in Lakota. The others joined in. I felt the unity of the prayer, a presence coming together at our center. It gathered at the fire and then shot up, *woooosht,* opening a space. There was almost a light to it, a wind, directed up by the collective. The energy seemed fueled by an amalgam of our prayers, a oneness.

We left the tent, heading into the cool late night, the fresh clean air, under an open sky bright with stars.

When I got up in the morning, Jane handed me a mug of coffee, kissed my cheek, and left for work. Just before I got back in the rental car and drove to the airport, I called to check in at home. Phil didn't pick up, so I dialed into our voicemail machine. There was one message, left late the previous night, after Jane and I had left the *inipi*. My heart raced. Was something wrong with my parents? Or Phil's? Why hadn't he called me? Throat tight, I pressed "1" to hear the message, barely breathing as I listened to an unfamiliar woman's voice. It was Sophie, the rabbi's daughter, calling from Russia.

"We have found your child," she said. A baby boy, six months old, soon of legal adoption age in Russia, had been located at an orphanage in St. Petersburg.

SOME WEEKS LATER, we received a video of a joyous little baby boy, happily gesticulating, raising his arms, smiling at a nurse. *"Da, da,"* he cooed in Russian. Yes, yes. He was pure love. He radiated it, a high-voltage, laser love. A soaring euphoria consumed me, a love so immediate and powerful it moved through me like a tide, miraculous. I was carried and held.

Phil and I went to bed that night as parents. In the deep of the night, the presence came again—that full sense in the air, the numinous light. *If you were pregnant now,* it asked, *would you still adopt?*

"Yes!" I said. Tears brimmed my eyes. Of course I would still adopt. I had already met our son. I was madly in love with him. "Yes!" I cried again.

Phil stirred and woke. I embraced him.

"Let's name him Isaiah," I said. It's a Hebrew name; it means *Yahweh (God) is salvation.* "Isaiah Lakota."

"Yes," he said, laughing, kissing me.

That night we conceived.

CHAPTER 9

THE CASTLE AND THE WAVE

The science that I knew simply couldn't explain my story. It didn't answer why a group of women praying for their sons in South Dakota helped me find a child in Russia the same night, or how my body was suddenly able to do on its own what it had been struggling in vain to do for five years. I was in awe of the mystery. And I hungered to know the how and why of what had happened.

At the same time, I was working professionally to understand why and how personal spirituality is so protective against depression and other forms of mental suffering. What is the seat of spirituality in our lived, daily experience? In our bodies? Brains? Awareness? Why does it have such a robust impact on our mental wellness? It seemed to me that the protective benefit comes because when you engage spiritual awareness, you see, feel, and walk through life in a different way. But could we see that kind of awareness physiologically? And could we help patients access it intentionally?

I didn't yet know how to push these questions forward, but

little by little, our understanding of the physiology of depression was deepening. Susan Nolen-Hoeksema, a senior colleague at Yale, who had also earned her doctorate with Marty Seligman at the University of Pennsylvania years ahead of me, was now a leading expert on the link between depression and certain patterns of thinking. In trying to understand why women are twice as likely as men to experience depression, she had discovered that women tend to rely more on a cognitive process called rumination—mental spinning or overthinking—to cope with negative moods. While men generally engage in activities that distract them from their bad moods, women tend to dwell on the causes and consequences of their moods, asking, *Why am I feeling this way? Why can't I handle things better? What's wrong with me?* This tendency to ruminate—to go down a rabbit hole of unrelenting thoughts and questions—only worsens a depressed mood, in part because the negative content of the thoughts reinforces the negative mood, but also because the process of rumination is passive and repetitive. Although people generally engage in rumination because they want to achieve new insights about themselves or their situation, Susan found that the effects of rumination are rarely positive for people who are already depressed—it impairs problem solving, deters social support, and fuels a brooding sense of low self-worth.

For example, in one study Susan randomly assigned rumination or distraction tasks to depressed and non-depressed participants. Those assigned rumination tasks were asked to spend eight minutes thinking about the meanings, causes, and consequences of their current feelings: *Think about the level of motivation you feel right now. Think about the long-term goals you have set. Think about what your feelings might mean.* When prompted to ruminate, depressed participants went into an emotional tailspin. They talked in a negative tone, recalled bad childhood memories, discussed upsetting life events and personal problems, and launched into self-blame and self-criticism. They were also more susceptible to external criticism. In a follow-up experiment, when the depressed ruminators were given negative feedback on a reading comprehension test, they took longer to complete the next reading assignment, and remembered less of what they'd read, suggesting that rumination disrupts our attention, focus, motivation, and ability to implement solutions. None of these negative outcomes occurred for the non-depressed participants who were asked to ruminate, or for the depressed participants who were given an eight-minute distraction task—to visualize the layout of the post office, or think about a boat slowly crossing the Atlantic, or visualize clouds forming in the sky.

Susan found that depression reinforces rumination; and rumination reinforces depression. Perhaps this feedback loop helped explain what our field called the "kindling" hypothesis, the idea that while initial lifetime episodes of depression or other mood disorders are typically associated with major life stresses—such as divorce or loss—later recurrences of depression are less likely to be associated with a specific life event. The later depressive episodes seem to come out of nowhere, without a major life event as a catalyst. Molehills become mountains. And with each depressive episode, the threshold for experiencing depression drops. In other words, it takes less and less of a trigger for depression to recur. It's as though the first bout of depression ignites a fire that rages more quickly and fiercely when less significant fuel—mere kindling—is thrown in. Depression might start as a single response to a difficult life event, but over time it becomes a go-to response.

I wanted to develop a spiritual awareness psychotherapy that could counter the kindling of depression in the brain by tapping us into the spiritual awareness Kenneth Kendler had shown we're hardwired to experience.

WHAT ELEMENTS WOULD spiritual awareness psychotherapy include? My own journey to motherhood gave me some of the basic principles that had guided me from a place of depression and discouragement to a place of hope and connection. I'd come into spiritual awareness—a way of toggling between different kinds of information and experience. Synchronicities had taught me to notice what was coming into my awareness or field of vision and to lean into what life was showing me. I'd experienced a personal relationship with a surprising transcendent presence. And I'd shifted away from the mentality of trying to fix the world to fit my preference and desire, and into a mental framework through which the world appeared loving and guiding. Most important, I sensed that I was in dialogue with that loving, guiding universe—that we were in an ongoing conversation. It wasn't a transactional relationship: *I say what I want, and I get it.* It was a collaborative relationship, an integration of inner and outer life, a way of tuning into, receiving, and emanating consciousness. I'd awakened to being in a relationship with life.

I began working with patients in an intentionally spiritually supportive way, discovering together their direct witness of what life was showing them and where the doors were being opened. In 2004, the American Psychological Association invited me to Chicago to demonstrate my spiritual awareness psychotherapy treatment model in a single session with a patient that would be recorded as part of a video series for practitioners.

My patient was Bev, a mother of five, in her fifties, at a difficult professional crossroads. For nine years she'd served as assistant director of a children's welfare nonprofit, and she was now in the final stretch of interviews to become director of the same organization.

"Do I really want it?" she asked. "I think I really want it." But she had doubts. "This could really happen. Am I prepared for it if it does?" A wistful smile passed across her face. "Am I prepared for it if it doesn't?"

She was at a crucial decision point, a time when our heads and our hearts hold the answer. In this culture, most of us are trained and socialized to rely on our heads when we're at a crossroads—to sort through the data and "make up our minds." But in the treatment framework I was developing, life itself holds the answers, and we make our best decisions when we integrate our heads, hearts, and life's guidance, learning to tune into our choices and hurdles as part of our spiritual path.

"What would it mean for you to become the director of your organization?" I asked Bev. "How do you experience the possibility of this coming through?"

She said that up until this point, her pursuit of the job had been a series of tasks—preparing her résumé and documentation, going through the initial interviews. She was performing tasks, checking off boxes, "going and going and going toward that direction." Now she was probing her goal.

"Is it really what I want to do?" she asked. "What am I going to view as the success?" She laughed. "I guess I'm questioning myself about why I'm questioning my ability to take that position."

She was on a mental treadmill, going around and around. I asked her to lean into the questions. What was at the heart of her dilemma?

"I'm not questioning whether the job is appealing or whether I can do it," she said.

The doubts that were surfacing, now that the job was within reach, were about the sacrifice of time away from her family. She'd gone back to college when her youngest child was two, and while she was proud of her educational and professional success, she knew that her absence had impacted her children. Now her oldest children were grown, with kids of their own, and on the surface the timing was perfect for her to pursue a professional advance and a new challenge. Yet something was preventing her from seamlessly embracing the opportunity.

"With the other children, when they are in the house, there is a felt sense of being close, of *blending*. I just don't feel that sense of blending with my youngest. She feels separate from me. These next years are really our last chance to be close, before she graduates from high school and moves out. When do my children, especially my youngest, stop making sacrifices for my goals? Or, really, when do I?" she said, her voice thickening with tears.

When she began to cry, I knew we'd arrived exactly where we needed to be, at a place of great energy and tenderness. We were getting closer to what was really at stake for her in the decision. She had moved beyond the mental spinning and opened the door to other ways of knowing, to what her heart was telling her.

"I spend time and energy advocating for other people's children," she said. "I'm gone till eight or ten at night, catching up with life on the weekend. There's not a balance."

In particular, she worried for her youngest child, who was about to enter high school. "She's comfortable isolating herself, being self-reliant, and that makes me uncomfortable. She seems to be fine, but there's a struggle in me. I feel like I'm missing an important part."

She shook her head, as though to silence the ache of what she feared she was missing. "At the same time, isn't not taking this new opportunity a way of not honoring the sacrifices my family has already made for me to achieve this?"

She had landed in her head again, reaching for answers through a necessary yet limited way of knowing, and a mental framework that insisted there were right and wrong answers. I wanted to guide her back to her inner knowing, and to a place of curiosity, not castigation.

"Whatever you decide will be generously shared," I said. "They'll learn from you, whatever path you take. We've talked about what they didn't get while you were in school or working. What have they gotten from your returning to school and work?"

She was quiet a moment. Then her eyes lit up. She sat up straighter. "You can be whatever you want to be," she said. "The only obstacles are the ones you put there." Her voice grew fuller as she spoke, passion in her face. "I've really modeled what I believe, that it's never too late to do anything that's in your heart." With obvious pride she told me about one of her sons, who had chosen to go into military service instead of college, now had children, and felt that he'd made the wrong choice for him. "I told him, 'Take one class and find out!' All my children believe that it's safe to go back and try again. I see my sons encourage their female partners' growth and exploration, and give real value to their wants and needs for personal growth."

The full, bright clarity of this truth hung in the air for a moment before Bev lowered her eyes, her brow furrowing again with doubt. She hadn't yet resolved her burning question, and I could sense how burdened she felt.

"Are you feeling any help from the universe on this decision?" I asked. "Any signs or suggestions?" This was the pivotal question, asking her to tune into her inner knowing.

"Oh, I want it all, I want it now," she said. "I want the answer to come."

She reminded me of myself, diligently scheduling another IVF treatment, doggedly pressing my way toward motherhood, tightly holding on to my goal. I wanted to open her to receiving the support from life she so craved.

"What's the message you'd like to have been hearing?" I asked.

She opened her mouth as though to respond, then paused. "I feel . . . ," she began, and faltered. "I feel like I'm a little out of tune with reading the universe. I'm feeling alone in this right now." Tears rose again. "There hasn't been a safe place to say that I'm not sure I want this." Her voice was quiet, as though the words rose from a seldom-accessed part of herself.

"I want to win the position," she said. Her voice rose with confidence. "I want to have that, to feel that I've accomplished that personal goal for me."

" 'With my youngest,' " I said. "That's where I heard the emotion earlier. Does it hurt?"

Crying, she nodded.

I leaned in and spoke softly. "What do you want?"

"Both," she said. "I cherish my children, and I was someone before I was their mother. I'm someone in addition to being their mother. To negate that negates me."

She looked at me, and in her searching glance I could see both her deepest wish and the weight of the impasse.

"You know," I told her, "oftentimes on the spiritual path there's a carrot, the thing we think we want *so much*. And when we have it, it vanishes. It wasn't really the carrot we needed. It was the journey."

I asked her to tell me more about the sense of loss and mourning she felt around her youngest daughter.

"I don't have the relationship with her I've had with my other children. Chitchat over mundane things, sharing dreams, seeking counsel. It's not that she doesn't have questions. It's that she doesn't know I'm available."

"If you were to not take the job and instead spend the next four years with your youngest, what would you want to teach your children about that? What would you want them to know?"

She inhaled sharply. "That happiness begins within." She sat quietly, as though letting her own words sink in. "I might have the position and the name tag. But your soul has to be at peace." Tears ran down her face.

I sensed her emotion as an opening awareness to the significance of her spiritual path, a marker of the intensity and value of her journey toward her own truth.

"She's going to be grown and gone in four years," Bev said through her tears. "I'd have such tremendous loss if she were to leave and things were still as they are between us. I feel she'd go into her adulthood not knowing that I was available for her, not in terms of need, but in that whole and spiritual way. This is my last opportunity to fix what's been missing between us since very early on."

It wasn't the answer she thought she wanted, or the answer she thought she was supposed to want. But she'd found and listened to what her inner voice was saying, the unacknowledged truth that had been holding her back, preventing her from moving forward, keeping her on a mental treadmill of doubt and indecision. In learning to listen with a full and open heart to the opportunities and losses in both directions, she'd found her own path. Through a climate of love and acceptance, without truncating or denying the process, we learn to tune into our spiritual awareness. We discover that we are seekers rather than makers of our path. In a secular, materialist world, we make meaning. But in my developing spiritual awareness framework, meaning is *revealed* and we interact with it. We are in dialogue with life. And our times of doubt, struggle, and depression often serve as portals to our awakened life.

This was a real departure from conventional treatment models. We were trained to diagnose and fix our patients. I was discovering the therapeutic benefit of tuning into how patients reveal the world.

AT THE TIME, there were two major hurdles in healing mental illness: diagnosis and treatment. These challenges are still with us today. Some of the lead creators of the American Psychiatric Association's *Diagnostic and Statistical Manual of Mental Disorders* (*DSM-5*) wrote an article on "inter-diagnostician reliability." They found that when two qualified practitioners diagnose a patient with a mental health disorder, their diagnoses often differ wildly. The degree of unreliability depends on the condition. For example, in diagnosing schizophrenia, their diagnoses correlated about eight to nine times out of ten; for non-manic bipolar disorder, six to seven times out of ten. But when someone is diagnosed with major depressive disorder, nearly 70 percent of the time the patient would not receive the same diagnosis from a different practitioner. The agreement between diagnoses is even less for the types of depression that lack clear start-and-stop episodes, or involve a mix of common symptoms such as anxiety. The symptoms and expressions of mental health conditions show up in different ways in different people. And the conditions appear different depending on who's looking at them. One-third of patients visiting a general psychiatric practice will not receive a reliable principal diagnosis at the first visit.

We lack precision and effectiveness in how we identify these prevalent and painful conditions—and also in how we treat them. Despite the fact that only half of treated patients see a disappearance of symptoms within a year of seeking treatment, more and more people are medicated for mental illness. About one in ten Americans from middle school through adulthood take antidepressants. This rate is even higher for middle-aged women: 23 percent—nearly one-quarter—of women aged forty to fifty-nine take antidepressants. The sizable increase in medication is doing little to curb the global surge in depression and anxiety.

The high medication rates are especially baffling when we consider that less than one-third of people taking an antidepressant have seen a mental health professional in the past year, and that more than two-thirds of people taking antidepressants do not meet the criteria for a major depressive disorder. SSRIs are being used as a palliative for life, and while they improve the symptoms of low mood, they don't treat the root cause of distress. We have become a mass-medicating culture. It's failing to heal us—and in some cases, it's making us worse. Antidepressants taken during pregnancy increase the risk of autism and compromised brain structure and connectivity in the baby. And young adults taking high-dose antidepressants such as Prozac and Seroxat have nearly double the risk of suicidal behavior.

If we could understand with greater and greater specificity how depression and anxiety—and their shield, spirituality—behave in the brain, we'd be better able to diagnose patients and offer targeted treatments that are lasting, not palliative; that treat causes, not symptoms; that offer more powerful protection with far fewer risks. We could even get ahead of the game with prevention and different school-based approaches to whole-child development, offering the possibility that the next generation could suffer less, and benefit from seeing life more fully.

But we were still some years away from the highly refined imaging tools and statistical techniques that would afford us nuanced glimpses of the workings of the brain. Unable to pursue my questions about spirituality in our neuroanatomy and physiology, I continued exploring spiritual awareness in clinical settings, focusing in particular on depression and anxiety as portals to awakening.

KATHLEEN MCKINLEY SAT in my office one morning, petite and elegant, impeccably dressed in designer clothes, something sharp and exacting in her heart-shaped face and green eyes. Her blond hair was shot through with gray. She was stunning and commanding, yet also pained and remote. She appeared to be disoriented, as though her power had unraveled. When she spoke, tears filled her eyes.

"I'm living my worst fear made real," she said.

Her husband, an acclaimed film director, had just told her he'd been having an affair with one of his costume designers. He was in love, and he wanted a divorce.

"I tried so hard to protect our children from a broken world," Kathleen said, wiping tears from the gentle creases at the corners of her eyes.

An accomplished journalist who had traveled extensively, Kathleen had put her professional ambitions on the back burner to raise two children and support her husband as he launched his career. Her most important life goal was to give her children a better childhood than she had experienced. Her parents had fought constantly, divorced when she was young, and gone on to struggle with alcoholism and the demands of new families. Kathleen had grown up distant from them. They weren't abusive, but she had felt their distraction and neglect, and had worked hard as an adult to repair the feeling of being inadequate and unloved. She gave everything to her own family—always seeking the best teachers and opportunities for her children, the finest quality of everything, giving her kids the ideal life of which she had felt deprived in her own childhood. Her son was now in high school, her daughter finishing elementary school; both kids excelled in music and athletics. But she was afraid the rift in her marriage would destroy their happiness and security.

"The world they know just disappeared," she said.

"What about you?" I asked. "What does this divorce mean for you?"

She gripped the arms of her chair and then lifted a hand to her chest. "I don't know," she said. "It's strange, but I don't know. I've always known what I want. But now I don't."

Her anxiety ran deeper than her husband's betrayal, deeper than her sense of abandonment. Her fear was about how to land in the world. The thing she had strenuously sought to protect herself and her children from had come true. So how was the world built? How would she navigate it? What was life—her life—really about?

These were spiritual questions. And hers was a classic midlife situation. The old way cracks open. It no longer holds. Or it's no longer enough. This experience is so familiar in our culture that we give it a name—midlife crisis—and recognize its symptoms: affairs, sailboats, sports cars, cavalier business decisions, the impulsive pursuit of something newer, better, fuller before time runs out. I've learned to call it midlife *chaos*. The world gets rearranged. Often, it's the things we've hidden from or tried most to control—our deepest fears and vulnerabilities—that assert themselves in midlife. We might discover that the things we've counted on as our bedrock have crumbled, or that our choices have led us further and further from our true goals and desires. Like Kathleen, we're jolted out of the status quo and into a reckoning, an understanding that our customary way of dealing with life's uncertainties—trying to control the outcomes—is no longer working.

What was my role as her guide? How could I help her to transcend her state of crisis and nightly panic attacks, to change her perception that she was alone and unlovable, that she had failed her kids?

The top treatment models of the day—forms of cognitive behavioral therapy—teach that our anxiety and suffering come from our misguided thoughts and underlying schemas of the world. We have habitual ways of making meaning and ordering the world—and sometimes the way we think about others and ourselves is askew. We heal by learning to identify and then change our damaging habitual thoughts. If I used classic CBT with Kathleen, I would help her examine and transform her underlying beliefs—about love, safety, self-worth.

The problem with CBT is that while it can enhance our self-esteem and help us feel more uplifted and hopeful, it doesn't offer us a bigger life or bigger view of the world. We might feel better about ourselves, but we're still stuck in a self-referential, "little me" world. As Susan Nolen-Hoeksema's work on rumination had so beautifully shown, women who are depressed are capable of having positive thoughts—but they feel the benefits of these positive thoughts less intensely than women who aren't depressed. And they don't disengage the tight hold of rumination.

Traditional CBT could help Kathleen change her thoughts—but not her lens. She would still be seeking growth and healing within a self-referential framework. I wanted to help Kathleen heal in that deeper, transformative way—to ignite the protection and power of awakening and fuel the big blast of healing that comes when spiritual awareness reshuffles the meaning we make from our lives.

I asked Kathleen to take stock of the chaos. We started in her body. She described the burn of anger in her chest, the dizzy, churning sensation of free fall in her gut, as though the earth had dropped out from under her. Then I asked her to take me into her home. She mentally walked me through the rooms, showing me the cereal bowls in the sink—she no longer felt like cooking— and the empty hangers on her husband's side of the closet, the untouched pillow on his side of the bed. She cried as she described her son's anger and her daughter's despair, the way they looked at her with sorrow and concern, her daughter's bedroom light turned on all night because she was suddenly afraid of the dark. She described the half-finished jigsaw puzzle on the dining room table, her kids' stacks of schoolbooks on the living room floor, how instead of retreating to their rooms to do homework, they preferred to stay together till bedtime, sprawling near her on the rug or the couch.

Kathleen suddenly opened her eyes and looked at me in surprise. "My worst fear came true," she said. "But we're fine. Our family broke. And it didn't destroy us."

The following week I asked her to take stock of the old life, the one she'd been so terrified to lose. As she examined the textures and patterns, the limitations of the old life popped into relief. She'd given up the journalism career she loved. She'd stopped traveling. She'd stopped spending time with friends.

"I was always so busy," she said, "but I'm not sure why. What was I doing? Obsessing and running around for complete minutiae." She shook her head. "The first time my son took the ACT, he got a thirty-five. It's a great score. But I spent all summer shuttling him around to tutors and classes so he could try for a perfect thirty-six. And for what? He didn't get to be a camp counselor. He couldn't go on a fishing trip up in Maine with his grandfather. I was so anxious about success and survival. And the whole time I was racing around trying to make every detail perfect, the life I *thought* was safe wasn't really safe."

She realized her marriage had become painful and problematic long before the divorce. For years she'd been frozen and numb. And afraid.

"I think for a long time I had a feeling this was coming," she said. "On some level I sensed it, and ignored it. Withdrew, shuttered myself away to try to avoid being hurt."

With a chill, I remembered the dream I'd had the night before I learned our baby's heart was stopped. How I'd tried to erase the dream, to shove my inner knowing back into the darkness, to cling to what I *wanted* to be true. Everything else in my life that I'd wanted to outwardly control or accomplish, I'd gotten. I had the degrees I wanted, the career I wanted, the marriage and friends I wanted. Then it turned out that the one thing I really cared about, that really mattered, I couldn't control or plan for. For years I hadn't known how to release my tight grip— how to stop trying to will or force reality to be what I wanted it to be.

Kathleen began to do what had eluded me. As the months passed, she discovered that the betrayal and loss and uncertainty of the divorce hurt terribly, but not as much as the blind, narrow way she'd been choosing to live before things fell apart. Now she had fuller vision, and she was building a new map of reality. She saw things differently through her new lens. I asked her to notice what was catching her eye now, to examine the things life was showing her that might take her by surprise.

"I'm taking more action," she said. "Reaching out, getting support from people near and far who'd fallen off the radar."

Another day she exclaimed, "All these people are showing up! It feels like love is everywhere. People carry love."

About six months after she'd begun treatment, she got a call, out of nowhere, for a new job at an advocacy group that helped women in need. "I didn't even apply!" she said. "I feel so supported, like the world is taking care of me."

As Kathleen felt more held and guided by life, she began to recognize how her own behavior had contributed to the dissolution of her marriage. Her husband had done the worst of it—but she'd played a part too.

"I was so afraid of not being loved and of being alone, I acted out of meanness sometimes," she said. "I pushed him away."

She'd made preemptive strikes to protect herself against feeling unloved, but they had backfired.

"This is all a lesson for me about love," she said. "I couldn't see love. I annihilated love. But I was lovable all along. And it's a loving world."

As her awareness shifted, so did her behaviors. She took the job as a women's advocate, began to travel again, spent more time outside enjoying nature. She reconfigured the old systems she had used to measure her worth and accomplishment: finding the perfect piano teacher for her daughter, hosting the perfect dinner party, helping her son earn a perfect score on the ACT. She found enormous fulfillment in supporting and connecting with others, spending weekends at the ocean or in the mountains near the Finger Lakes, seeking out spiritual retreats.

"I'm a spiritual person, and I always have been," she said. "But I buried it deep inside. I borrowed my husband's view that spirituality isn't serious, that there's no evidence. But my grandmother was spiritual, and now I sense that certainty within me, too—that I'm fine in the world, that I'm not alone, that things work out."

By the end of Kathleen's treatment, much was the same on the surface. She was still living in Pelham, New York (though in a different house), still completely devoted to her children's well-being. But something within had shifted. She had moved away from her old patterns—of worry, of appealing to her husband's authority and expertise, of trying to make her life conform to what she thought it "should" be, trying to avoid whatever might hurt—to a way of being in which she met life as it was. And she came to see her husband's affair, the crisis situation that had brought her into therapy, completely differently.

Before the divorce, living with the perception that it was up to her alone to make her life a certain way, she couldn't experience the fundamental unity of life. She was isolated and stressed, striving for control. And though she was devoted and committed to her family, she was stuck within a utilitarian view of relationships, striving to determine *what others did to me,* or *what others can do for me.* Her role as wife and mother was all about creating a sense of security, trying to bring about the love and safety she had so yearned for in her own life. She had beautiful intentions. But she lived them out within a transactional view of relationships, and her husband's affair and abandonment left her feeling intensely alone and apart, reinforcing her conception of love as something you have or don't have.

As she healed, she began to experience the presence of love in the fabric of life, and to feel life acting with her on her behalf.

"Now I sense a certainty within me," she said a year after her initial visit. "That I'm fine in the world, that I'm not alone, that things work out."

She looked at me in wonder and surprise.

"I never could have predicted that his leaving me would become my get-out-of-jail-free card," she said. She never would have left him, she never would have chosen a different life. But the divorce was exactly what she needed to open her life up again.

"My whole life I thought my job was to build this perfect

sandcastle and keep it safe," she said. "But when the castle finally fell apart, I could suddenly see everything beyond it—the beach, the ocean, the waves."

The waves come and the castle crumbles. We experience loss, trauma, suffering. We get the things we're most terrified of, the things we least want. Even when we're bent on protecting the castle, we can't prevent the tides. And when we cling too tightly to our desire for control, anything can break us—we're so brittle, fragile, ready to collapse and fall that any risk feels too severe, any block insurmountable. We are so consumed by our need to do things right, that we lose sight of the larger meaning for what we do and are blind to the regeneration that loss makes possible.

CHAPTER 10

A DIFFERENT LIFE

You're not going to believe this," my friend and fellow researcher Dr. Suniya Luthar said one afternoon in 2008. We were sitting in her university office, cafeteria salads awkwardly balanced on our knees, meeting to discuss how to abate the significantly elevated rates of depression our field was seeing across the United States.

I'd known Suniya since I was an undergrad at Yale and she was the teaching assistant for my abnormal psychology class. Sitting in her class as a nineteen-year-old, I'd been inspired to see this lively, engaging woman, so radiant she practically sparkled, who was also an intense academic. With Suniya, there was never any small talk. Intelligent and intense, she looked at the world with laser focus. She was a scientist's scientist—following the trail of the numbers, striving to get to the bottom of a mystery or problem. Her early work on the intersection between poverty and mental health had contributed to the formation of Head Start programs, and had modeled the power of science to change and improve lives. Now she was a tenured professor of psychology at Columbia, still committed to doing research that supported the welfare of kids, especially teens growing up in under-resourced urban areas. Because rates of depression shoot up between the ages of twelve and eighteen, it was vital to focus on adolescents if we were to curb the growing epidemic.

As we crunched our bland lettuce, Suniya filled me in on the recent surprising turn in her research. She had been looking for a comparison group for the urban youth population she was studying, and had begun investigating upper-middle-class teens in affluent suburbs outside of New York City, San Francisco, and other major U.S. cities. But as she learned more about these affluent suburban comparison groups, she found that the "privileged" or "rich" kids were doing markedly worse in several measures than their less affluent peers. They had much higher rates of substance abuse, depression, and anxiety, and despite having resources and physical safety, felt more vulnerable and fearful.

The finding surprised many people in the field. By and large, the affluent kids had engaged and supportive parents, they went to highly ranked schools, they had the resources for enrichment activities and travel, they enjoyed many educational, professional, and social opportunities and never wanted for food to eat or safe streets to walk. Why were they so depressed?

By going into the schools and interviewing kids, Suniya had identified a social ecology that she thought explained their mental suffering. For one thing, the majority of affluent kids in her study had perceptions of contingent love from their parents and families. They said things like "My dad shows up at my soccer games, but not at family dinner," or "My mom asks me, 'How did you do on the math test?,' not 'How are you feeling?'" Many of the kids said they felt like commodities. Their job was to perform—academically, athletically, musically—and earn their parents' approval. Endless attention was paid to report cards and trophies and rankings. No one said, "I'm so happy to see you."

"If they're not achieving, they feel inadequate," Suniya said. "And if they *are* achieving, they're in a state of fear of not achieving. They're self-medicating by the droves just to try to ease this chronic anxiety about their worth."

A similar negative social ecology existed among their peer groups as well. When she studied the predictors of popularity, she found that for girls, the behaviors that went hand in hand with popularity were being skinny and using interpersonal aggression to establish dominance—essentially, being a "mean girl." For boys, it was substance abuse and exploitation of girls. Value was a measure of the number on the scale, the list of sexual conquests, a tally of wins and losses, accomplishments and failures.

Suniya was in the midst of a longitudinal study, tracking kids from adolescence to adulthood, from age twelve to twenty-four, and asked if I'd work with her and add some spirituality measures to the study.

A few years later, she and our grad student Sam Barkin came to my office at Columbia to share some initial findings.

They found that among the affluent youth, the rate of spirituality was significantly lower than in the population at large. Only 15 percent of the kids from highly resourced suburbs reported that they had a personal spiritual identity or practice—a rate of spirituality less than one-quarter the national rate published in Pew and Gallup polls.

They also found that the 85 percent of the sample who were not spiritual had over tenfold the national rate of risk for sociopathy. Socialized in a culture that equated their worth with how fat or skinny they were, or whether they got an A or a B on the last exam, they had no unconditional love or sense of connection as a bedrock. They'd grown up lonely and disconnected, using others and being used in an achievement game.

I stepped over the piles of books and papers on the floor of my office so I could look out the small window. Clouds shifted, and weak winter sunlight washed over the brick and concrete and bare trees. Students hurried between buildings, their backs hunched under heavy packs, heads hunkered down against the wind.

"There's more," Sam said. "The fifteen percent who do consider themselves spiritual are not experiencing the elevated, through-the-roof anxiety, depression, and substance abuse of the rest of the cohort."

The cross-sectional leg of the data didn't prove that spirituality *causes* better mental health. But, once again, it showed that spirituality strongly correlates with a reduced rate of suffering. That if you are spiritual, you are protected and inured from otherwise increased risk.

A few more years later, I saw the results on spiritual development and mental health for the kids Suniya had followed since age twelve who were now twenty-four, most of them finished with college and on to jobs or graduate school. We saw that those who were high in spirituality at age eighteen, even if they experienced doubt and depression during college, emerged on the other side with strong spirituality. These young adults, who'd been spiritual as eighteen-year-olds and had maintained or renewed their spiritual life in their twenties, were much less likely to be depressed, much less likely to abuse substances, and more likely to be in healthy relationships and to join organizations or communities of contribution. A strong spiritual core gave these young people a whole different life.

.   .   .

I WANTED TO explore how our lives unfold differently with spirituality, and together with my colleague Myrna Weissman, whose data I'd used in my study on intergenerational transmission, I developed a long-term clinical course data analysis to examine the relationship between spirituality and depression during emergence into adulthood.

The sixteen-year-olds who'd been my second-generation sample in the intergenerational transmission study were now twenty-six. We focused on two measurements across the decade: depression and spiritual formation. Using a structured clinical interview called the Schedule for Affective Disorders and Schizophrenia—Lifetime, we determined who in the sample met criteria for major depressive disorder. And to discern spiritual formation, we asked the tried-and-true question about the personal importance of religion or spirituality. Of all the ways we might measure spirituality, this question remained the best, I think because it cut straight to a person's daily lived sense of spiritual awareness. A change in response from age sixteen to twenty-six helped us see the strengthening or atrophy of a spiritual core over time.

Given the earlier epidemiological findings on the protective benefits of spirituality, we anticipated that young adults with a strong personal spirituality would be less likely to have experienced depression. But two striking findings emerged.

First, those who had strong personal spirituality at age twenty-six were *two and a half times more likely* to have been depressed in the past. In other words, spiritual formation doesn't seem to be an alternative to depression so much as a way of being that emerges alongside or through struggle.

Second, those who had strong spirituality by age twenty-six were *75 percent protected* against a recurrence of major depression for the next ten years. And for those who were highly spiritual and had gone through major depression in the past, the protective benefit of spirituality against a recurrence of depression was even higher: a striking *90 percent*. These were people at high familial risk for depression, who'd grown up in households shrouded in a rain cloud of depression. When they experienced painful losses, disappointments, or unwanted experiences in their late adolescence and early adulthood, they seemed conditioned for a spiritual response. It was as though their sensitivity to and familiarity with mental suffering enhanced their capacity to marshal a deeper spiritual response to life challenges. High-risk people who built a spiritual muscle to respond to suffering were protected against the downward spiral the next time sorrow or disappointment came around, because they had cultivated a spiritual response.

I realized that my initial understanding of the epidemiological data—that spirituality is a protective factor against mental suffering—was a bit broad. The new finding suggested that spiritual awareness doesn't buffer against ever facing suffering so much as suffering pulls spiritual awareness forward, building the spiritual core that prepares us for the next time we face suffering. It appeared that grappling with moments of pain and emptiness actually catalyzed spiritual formation in some way.

I thought of my own depression as an undergrad, and of my caseload of university students who were going through developmental depression. Could it be that we have a spiritual biological clock that plunges us into despair, disorientation, anger, sorrow, depression, and that through asking questions and feeling the emptiness and fear of being disconnected or having no purpose in life, we reach a deeper connection with life? Just like we get gray hair at a certain point, or become able and then unable to bear children, might the possibility of spiritual deepening be written into our physiological development? It seemed possible that our biology gives us an augmented capacity for spiritual perception at certain life phases. Our study showed that if we respond to the surge of our spiritual life booting up, we are set up for the next phase of life. If we don't, we're more likely to be depressed—to have an ongoing hunger for love, connection, and transcendence that we don't know how to marshal.

We can choose how we approach life, especially during major inflection points—adolescence, midlife, times of loss or trauma. We can ignore the existential questions, and the booting-up of our spiritual awareness. We can medicate with pharmaceuticals that dull the pain of the questions, or with substances that give us a temporary reprieve—or a synthetic version of the transcendence we long for. Or we can open the door to a reshuffling of meaning, to the foundational, felt awareness that we are loved and held and part of it all.

I thought of a high school student I'd met when I was conducting interviews in very well-resourced areas similar to those in Suniya's studies. I'd sat in Hannah's tidy bedroom in her family's elegant Colonial home in the suburban New York area, discussing the ins and outs of high school life. A dancer with a five-days-a-week training schedule, Hannah was animated and graceful. She also showed signs of anxious depression. Her nails were bitten down to the quick, the skin on her fingers raw and bleeding in places. As she spoke about her daily life and perspective, I noticed her toggling in and out of spiritual awareness, between a fractured and connected way of being.

"Girls my age are so critical of their bodies," she said. "How much they weigh, how they look." She shook her head and laughed. "I'm comfortable in my body, but I still spend forty-five minutes in the morning doing my hair and putting on my makeup! It's not like I roll out of bed and think, 'Yep, I probably look good today.'"

I asked her to say more about the insecurity she noticed in herself and others. Where did it come from?

"Judgment is just in the culture," she said. "If you're a boy, you make snarky comments about girls. You say things like 'She's really let herself go.' And if you're a girl you examine all your flaws. My friends are always saying things like 'I used to have such a good butt, but now you can't tell, my thighs are so huge. I need to stop eating,' or 'I have no curves. I have a boy body and I'm so disproportionate.' You look in the mirror and the first thing you think is 'I'm disgusting.'"

She said that her teachers and parents also had misguided expectations of kids. It was hard for her to figure out what she wanted to do in her life—her mind was so crowded with other people's critiques and demands.

"Have you ever felt spiritual?" I asked.

She nodded emphatically and smiled. "Yes! When I'm in nature or just outside, appreciating a beautiful moment. One time my family was at the shore on vacation and I was standing at the ocean's edge, just looking out. Suddenly I had this feeling—*I am like a wave.* I can't really describe it. It felt slow, like a slo-mo movie, all dreamy and fluid, and then, *boom,* I was connected to something bigger. I thought, 'I'm here. I feel like I'm *just me.*' It doesn't happen very often, but when it does, I feel so much smarter. Like anything is possible. I love it!" She smiled again, then shrugged. "But it's not scientific. And I believe in science and evolution and everything."

I was struck by how effortlessly she had called up a spiritual experience, how intuitively she'd known what I meant, and how buoyantly she described it. And how quick she was to offer a disclaimer. She expressed awe—and then disavowed it. Somewhere along the way, Hannah had been taught that this spiritual state of being was not fully real—that it didn't really count.

The new data showed that her life would unfold very differently depending on whether she cultivated or dismissed her spirituality. If she could embrace and deepen that sense of transcendent unity she'd experienced at the shore, she wouldn't be prone to depression later in life. If she silenced her spiritual self, depression was more likely to return.

TOGETHER, THE FINDINGS from my three epidemiological studies showed that the protective benefits of spirituality were incontrovertible, and as clear as counting beans, no interpretation necessary. But the results were based on broad, two-dimensional data, from a 10,000-foot aerial view. I would need to get much closer to the body and the brain to understand more, to explain the pattern. The self-report data sets, while good at painting a broad picture of our human condition, didn't point to anything concrete to do for patients. As a clinician, I had been exploring what spiritual development actually entails, and how clinicians can teach or guide our patients toward spiritual awareness. As a researcher, I needed to understand if the relationship between spirituality and psychological health could be seen at a material level. Were depression and spiritual development in fact expressions of a common physiology? Building on Kenneth Kendler's discovery that spirituality is innate, was it possible to find the biological mechanism of our spiritual capacity—further evidence of spirituality in our bodies, brains, or genes?

CHAPTER 11

WIRED FOR SPIRITUALITY

In 2009, researchers at my colleague Dr. Brad Peterson's lab at Columbia began asking the questions about depression that I was asking about spirituality: Is there a physiological foundation for depression? Is it visible in the brain? Brad and his team posited that an established path of depression might be visible—that there might be not only specific brain activity but also specific brain structures associated with depression and other mood disorders and mental illness. In an amazing contribution to the field, Brad's lab used neuroimaging techniques to examine the brain structures of 131 people in Myrna Weissman's extensive data sample. The subjects ranged in age from six to fifty-four. Half had a family history of depression, while the other half were at low risk.

The subjects with parents and grandparents who'd experienced depression showed significant—up to 28 percent—*relative thinness in the brain's right cortex*. The outermost surface of this region of the brain was much thinner in people at high risk for depression. Brad said that what he considered most extraordinary about the finding was that "you're seeing it two generations later, and you're seeing it in both children and adults. And it's present even if those offspring themselves have not yet become ill."

He said the cortical thinning wasn't necessarily a familial genetic trait—that it could be "a consequence of growing up with parents or grandparents who are ill. Studies have shown that when parents are depressed, it changes the environment in which children are growing up."

The region of thinning—the cerebral cortex—is where we process emotional stimuli. Specifically, this part of the brain is important to reasoning, planning, and mood. A thinner cortex inhibits our ability to perceive and orient in the world, and see ourselves clearly. Brad's team showed in a material, physiological way what we had only known before in a clinical sense: that depression goes hand in hand with a narrowing of the perceptual field, and a distortion in our sense of relationship with others and the larger world—the mind going round and round, failing to see the bigger view.

If there were visible biological pathways of depression, could there also be biological pathways of spirituality?

IN 2011, a unique and unexpected opportunity came my way. My longtime colleague Myrna—who had generously shared her intergenerational data with me and Brad—had gone to the John Templeton Foundation, an organization that supports scientific discovery in pursuit of answers to "the big questions." Drawing on the award they'd given for the epidemiology paper I'd developed with her team, she asked if they might be interested in funding her lab to look at the neural correlates of depression. They offered the funding—and wanted to include the "spirituality and religion person"—me—as an investigator.

It was a dream come true. We'd have the rich data of Myrna's beautiful thirty-five-year study, a three-generation sample community that included people at high genetic risk for depression as well as people with deep spiritual lineages.

Myrna had been following the same cohort of New Haven women long enough that they'd had children and grandchildren. The oldest generation was my parents' age, and the second generation my age. Maybe we'd sat in the same coffee shops when I was in college there, or gone to see the same bands at Toad's Place. I felt a connection to the "G-2" group, because I had gone through developmental depression at the same time, in the same place, and, like many of these women, I'd had a process of spiritual emergence. I saw my story in their story, and I think that is what data sets always are to me: human stories. Now, for the first time, we had the funding and the research sample to investigate the relationship between depression and spirituality in the same cohort of women I'd been following for much of my life as a scientist.

Slowly, we established the design for the study. We decided to examine the occipital, parietal, and precuneus regions of the brain—regions other researchers had found to be associated with depression. The occipital lobe, located at the back of the head, is most commonly thought of as the brain's visual perception center; the parietal, a bit higher up, helps us orient ourselves within a field of sensory information; and the precuneus is the part of the parietal lobe used in reflection.

Focused on the brain's regions of perception, orientation, and reflection, we would take magnetic resonance imaging (MRI) scans of people at high and low genetic risk for depression, and compare and contrast the brain structures of high-risk participants who reported a strong personal spirituality and those who did not.

"What exactly do you think we'll find in there?" my colleagues warmly ribbed. "Do you *really* believe we'll see anything?"

I couldn't say. But the strength of the epidemiology data and the emerging imagery studies on depression suggested a possibility that our scanner research might also lead to a clear finding. And I trusted the numbers to show what was true.

But I was completely unprepared for what we saw on the day eighteen months into the study when the MRI team met to review the new findings—the day Ravi, the data analyst, passed out the composite images of the high-spiritual and low-spiritual brains and we had our first clear and breathtaking view of the awakened brain.

The subjects for whom spirituality and religion were highly important had a healthier neural structure than did those for whom spirituality and religion held medium, low, or no importance. As I gazed at the printout of what the MRI team would come to call the "red brain"—the high-spiritual brain, with its broad and pervasive regions of cortical thickness—I could see the material counterpart to what I'd discovered in the last twenty years of clinical and epidemiological work. The red brain had something to do with the buffering effect of spirituality, how some of us are more protected against depression when going through developmental windows of risk. How we can struggle and doubt in a way that deepens our spiritual awareness and determines how we see life and choose to engage in every moment.

The finding opened a new door in our understanding of the psyche. For spiritually aware people across faith traditions—and including those without a faith tradition—the brain appeared able to protect itself from the long-standing neurological structures of depression.

ONE OF MY favorite aspects of publishing findings in scientific journals is the process of peer review—the practice of sending articles that are being considered for publication to at least two scientists who perform external analysis. It's generally understood in the scientific community that *any* article is improved through collaboration, and that many articles might be strengthened by added analyses or revisions. Because our MRI study on the awakened brain was such breakthrough research, so far outside the mold of anything *JAMA Psychiatry* had ever published before, we had to be even more meticulous. Our study went through a complete second round of peer review to ensure that the rigorous analysis was exceptionally ironclad.

Peer review is always anonymous. The more profound or novel the finding, the more likely it will be reviewed by well-recognized, expert scientists at the top of their field. But it's essential for the scientific validation process that the analysis be about scientific method and data analysis, not personalities, cultural vogue, or even shared areas of scientific interests. The work is evaluated purely on the merit of science.

Yet I hadn't forgotten the furrowed brows when I'd presented at Grand Rounds fifteen years ago. Even rigorous scientists hadn't been able to see the data outside the lens of their biases about spirituality as a crutch or cultural artifact. Would our peer reviews come back with the admonition to look for a hidden variable to explain the red brain?

But the reviews came back full of completely scientific, clear-minded insights, raising minor points of clarification and additional statistical follow-ups. In response to one of our findings, that cortical thickening was greater among people with not only high but sustained spirituality—high spirituality over time—one reviewer asked, "Could you test whether cortical thickness protects against the level of symptoms of depression?" In other words, did the red brain protect not just against long-term, more severe diagnosis of major depression, but could it be sufficiently sensitive to ameliorate the daily mild to moderate symptoms of depression? We ran a new analysis using a depression scale to incorporate symptoms of depression, and found that cortical thickening was indeed protective against here-and-now more subtle levels of depressive symptoms, not just against periodic episodes of diagnostic depression. Without the pure scientific engagement of peer review, we might never have observed this truth.

Another reviewer noticed that the magnitude of the effect of cortical thickening was even greater in the high-risk group, and asked us to dig into this data point. Why did high-spiritual people at high familial risk of depression have greater cortical thickening than high-spiritual people at low risk for depression? My brilliant colleague Craig Tenke hypothesized that perhaps the high-risk brains were more sensitive to the impact of spirituality. It was a huge insight, that people most prone to depression might be more profoundly enriched by spirituality—that a sensitivity to depression existed alongside a sensitivity to spirituality, resulting in greater neuroanatomic strengthening. People at low risk for depression still benefited from spirituality. But for those at high risk for depression and cortical thinning, spirituality mattered even more. Perhaps these are our artists, writers, faith leaders, shamans, and musicians, particularly sensitive to experience.

Inspired by the new insights that came from the peer review process, our team decided to investigate one more aspect of the group at high genetic risk for depression. We had study participants come into the lab and simply relax with their eyes closed, an electroencephalogram (EEG) attached to the back of their heads, near the parietal region of the brain, the posterior area where they had shown enhanced cortical thickness. We used the EEG to measure the energy the brain gives off. The subjects with a strong personal spirituality gave off a wavelength from the back of the brain that measured as *high-amplitude alpha* (alpha is 8–12 Hz)—a wavelength that also emanates from the posterior brain of meditating monks in some forms of practice and, notably, is "jump-started" in people using SSRI medications to treat depression; for people on SSRIs, however, the posterior high-amplitude alpha wavelength disappears when they stop taking the SSRI. In our study, the high-amplitude alpha reading was even more pronounced among the participants who both had a strong personal spirituality *and* had recovered from a major depression. Once again, we saw an amazing intertwining of depression and spirituality in the brain.

The decades-long search was over and, at once, posed questions to open a new line of inquiry. We had located a glimpse of the awakened brain. We had discovered that the parietal region—toward the back of the head, roughly the place where the bottom of a baseball cap or a Jewish kippah rides—is essential to engaging our spiritual awareness. And we had discovered reverse kindling—the way the brain can buffer and defend against the stronghold of depression across generations and through the life span.

Depression and spirituality appeared to be two sides of the same coin, vastly different experiences that in fact share some significant physiology. I had long wondered from an epidemiological and clinical perspective if some types of depression might be a symptom of a person's craving for spirituality and a call for the spiritual self to awaken. Now we could see in a physiological, material way that spirituality is a consciousness for which all of our brains are wired; and that, long-term, the spiritually engaged brain is a healthier brain. Suddenly depression didn't look like an illness, at least not all the time. It looked like a sensitivity or perceptual capacity—a knock at the door for the opportunity of an awakened brain.

CHAPTER 12

THE TWO MODES OF AWARENESS

W e'd found where spirituality lives in the brain, and we'd seen the structural benefits of an awakened brain. Now I wondered, How do we activate our spirituality and engage its protective power in our brains and our lives? I wanted to try to see spirituality in the moment—as it's being experienced—to learn if we could identify the real-time neural workings of spiritual awareness.

Other labs around the world were beginning to use a functional magnetic resonance imaging (fMRI) technique to try to map human thoughts, feelings, and experiences to specific regions of the brain. Whereas MRI measures and locates radiofrequency signals emitted by hydrogen atoms in the body in order to create pictures of anatomy, fMRI maps real-time brain activity by measuring blood flow in the brain. Since blood flow increases in regions of the brain that are in use, an fMRI scan can detect changes in neuronal activity based on changes in blood flow across regions of the brain.

I found wonderful neuroimaging collaborators at Yale. Marc

Potenza and Rajita Sinha had done decades of previous research in the areas of stress and addiction. More recently, they had collaborated using Rajita's "in-scanner" method, drawn from evidence that when people retell a personal experience in rich detail, describing the experience elicits the same neural correlates as the experience itself. We wanted to adapt Rajita's personal narrative methodology to see the neural correlates of spiritual experiences in the fMRI scanner. The novel fMRI study translated the strong personal devotion findings from epidemiology, and the more recent findings of the structurally robust awakened brain, into live-action images inside the scanner. We worked together for a full year before ever collecting data to design an innovative study that could identify the neural correlates of spiritual experience by having participants tell three separate and detailed personal experiences while they were in the scanner: one of a stressful event, one of a relaxing event, and one of a spiritual experience.

GIVEN THAT LATE adolescence to early adulthood is a time of emergence for both spirituality *and* depression, we decided to bring in young adult participants, men and women between the ages of eighteen and twenty-seven. In telling all three narratives, participants were asked to be as detailed as possible—to explain where they were, who was there, what they were doing, how things looked, and what bodily sensations they experienced as the event unfolded.

About half of the personal spiritual narratives included a time of prayer or an experience at a religious service, often with an emphasis on sounds (bells, voices in song or prayer) and on the sensation of barriers between self and others, or self and world, melting away. Roughly the other half of the personal narratives didn't involve prayer or religious worship, but instead included moments of spiritual awareness in nature—on a beach or snowy mountaintop, by a pond at a city park. These narratives often included references to light and sky, and to a sense of unity between self and environment, such as "You are part of everything around you and it is all a part of you," or "You're linked with the trees, the rocks, the mountains, the sky," or "You are just a speck in the universe, yet the universe is all within you." A few of the spiritual narratives didn't involve prayer or nature but an experience of transcendence felt during a sporting event or while playing music. Again the emphasis was on the sensation of being absorbed by something larger—of going beyond the body and into the music or cheering crowd.

No matter whether the spiritual experience was secular or religious, whether it took place indoors or in nature, in solitude or with others, all of the spiritual narratives shared important themes and physical sensations. Physically, the participants felt warm, calm, energized, and more alive. Their hearts beat faster, their senses sharpened, their nagging thoughts disappeared. Emotionally, they experienced clarity, awe, openness, peace, and unity, and felt a powerful connection with, and sometimes an overwhelming love for, other people, a higher power, or their surroundings. Boundaries dissolved. It wasn't just that they felt a sense of ease or peace, or an absence of pain or agitation. It wasn't just that it was a nice day and the sun was out and the flowers smelled good and they felt happy. There was a specific meaning attached to the physical and emotional experience—a feeling of oneness with the environment or the divine; a sense of their own individual voice or identity or presence dissolving into something larger around or beyond them. They narrated direct, felt experiences of oneness—moments in which they had an awareness of moving from a point to a wave. And they narrated an attentional "pop" of awareness—moments of sudden guidance when a problem or conflict or question resolved in an insight or realization: "*and then* I realized that I'm held and God has a plan for me"; "*and suddenly* I knew that I'm part of all life, and that I will find my direction."

In contrast, the relax narratives were physically and emotionally neutral. Participants told about lying in bed under a warm duvet, reading or listening to music, lounging on a deck chair in the sun. These were pleasant experiences, but there was no specific meaning associated with them.

I'd predicted that the stress narratives would be about working toward a big accomplishment or overcoming a challenge—learning Mandarin, taking the LSAT. But every single one of the stress narratives—whether it involved an obsession with acquiring a specific job, position, or person; striving for a "golden carrot"; or battling an ego injury or moment of fear—was less about overcoming a challenge and more about pedaling hard for control in the face of uncertainty. *I must have that job, that date, that school admission. Will I get it? How will I get and keep what's most important to me? Will there be enough of it for me?* The stress seemed to come not from obstacle or conflict alone, but also from how the experience forced the person's sense of total control, mastery, or self-worth into question. The stress seemed to stem from the terror of not having or getting what the person most craved. In contrast to the spiritual and relaxed experiences, the stress narratives included physical sensations such as racing thoughts, waves of panic, clenched muscles, gritted teeth, heavy or sinking feelings in the stomach or chest, and an overall sense of being empty, drained, or hollow. While the spiritual narratives included a breakthrough of clarity or realization, a sudden rearrangement of meaning, the stress narratives had a stuck, spinning, ruminative quality. No new information was streaming in. No new insights were landing.

It was striking to read each participant's narratives back-to-back. The same person who felt extreme disconnection and uncertainty was also capable of feeling deep unity and clarity. I couldn't wait to see their brain activity as they listened to their own experiences in the scanner. Would we see any associations or patterns among the experiences of stress or spiritual awareness? And how would our findings compare with the brain networks that other labs had recently found to be associated with depression?

Two weeks after telling their stress, relax, and spiritual narratives, the participants returned to the lab and listened to recordings of their three stories while they were in the scanner. When I opened the e-files from the team, I could see the fMRI scans lit up in branches of red, blue, and yellow, representing circuits of connection in the brain.

During the stress experiences, the participants' brains showed high activation of the insula and striatum, the regions in the frontal lobe that serve as the brain's motivation and reward centers. If you place your hand directly on top of your head, you can locate the approximate position of the insula and striatum. These regions help us take action toward goals or rewards. But when they are overused, the insula and striatum are like a stuck gear, telling us, *Got to get it. Got to keep it. Got to make it happen.* Or, *Oh no, not enough, need more!* These are the regions where we experience feelings of craving and anxiety, and the neural networks that, when out of balance, drive us to addiction and substance abuse. All of the emotions present during the stress narratives—dread, fear, regret, anger, despair, uncertainty, helplessness, disconnection, a sense of being stuck or out of control, wanting to escape or disappear, an overdrive striving for more—were associated with heightened activity in the insula and striatum.

During the spiritual narratives, four clear patterns emerged.

First came a deactivation, a powering down of the default mode network, the "rumination box," the region that often stimulates incessant self-rumination during depression and draws us away from present moment perception. Seeing the lights go out along the default mode network was like a visual representation of the small, controlling, self-obsessed little self backing off, bowing out.

Then there were clear patterns of activation in the ventral attention network. Our brains have two attentional networks—dorsal and ventral—that interact in a dynamic way. The dorsal attention network is our top-down attention; it filters incoming sensory and perceptual information, and while this is helpful in keeping us focused on the task or goal at hand, it also filters out unintentional information. When this inhibitory filter is released, our ventral attention network, our bottom-up attention, takes over. We found that spiritual experiences engage the ventral attention network, making us available to information outside of our immediate conscious awareness or control, allowing us to receive unanticipated but personally meaningful perceptions. The ventral attention network is where we receive the sudden breakthroughs common among the spiritual narratives—those flashes of clarity and insight.

We also saw the frontotemporal network come online during spiritual experiences. This network is implicated in processing representations of others and relational bondedness, such as when we were held by our mother or when we embrace a romantic partner. This finding strongly suggests that a feeling of relational intimacy accompanies spiritual states. We also discovered subcortical engagement, implicated in processing positive and rewarding emotions such as love and bliss, distinct from the positive emotions of a relaxing experience.

Finally, we saw increased activation in the posterior cingulate cortex and reduced activation in the inferior parietal lobe, where we navigate perceived distinctions between self and others. The parietal is linked to two key cognitive functions: perceiving and representing the self and others in time and space; and attributing agency, with left parietal activity signaling an attribution of agency outside oneself. The fMRI findings showed that in a spiritual state, the parietal shifts from unrelenting strong use to a pulsing or moderating use. The engagement of the parietal is what causes the brain to perceive separation. In a spiritual experience, hard, fixed boundaries soften. As feelings of separateness diminish, we embrace sensations of transcendence and union. This pattern suggests that when we have a spiritual experience, our identification with our physical self becomes more relaxed and our perception of boundaries between ourselves and others becomes more diffuse. We enter into a less bounded and more expanded sense of self. We perceive we are part of a oneness.

Overall, our study revealed that spiritual experiences are visible in the brain in three significant ways:

- an involuntary reorientation of attention
- a sense of love or embrace consistent with intimate attachment or bonding
- a sense of self that is both distinct and part of the greater oneness

For the first time, we could see in the scanner that spiritual awakening involves self-transcendent awareness *and* relationship. And that spiritual experiences induce a feeling of unity or closeness *whether or not* the content is explicitly relational. When we get over ourselves, or out of ourselves, we have a feeling of connection. We go from being a point to being a wave.

We'd found the sites where that movement from point to wave happens—the sites of our connection to awakened awareness. **The ventral attention network is where we see that the world is alive and talking to us; the frontotemporal network is where we feel the warm, loving embrace of others and of life itself; and the parietal lobe is where we know that we matter, belong, and are never alone.**

Staring at the dispersions of color across the scans, it occurred to me that I was witnessing not only a representation of how we can feel better and safer in the world, the "small self" perspective dissolving into a more expansive and complete worldview. I was also watching the mysterious process by which poems, symphonies, and innovations are born—with presence to reality, openness to new perceptions and information, and the capacity to transform perceptions into ideas, insights, meaning, and action. We'd found the neural docking station of love, unity, and guidance.

Two truths struck me as particularly potent and significant. First, the moments of intense spiritual awareness were biologically identical whether or not they were explicitly religious, physiologically the same whether the experience occurred in a house of worship or on a forest hike in the "cathedral of nature." They had the same level of felt intensity and the same pathways of fMRI activation—the same functioning neural correlates. This proved that every single one of us has a spiritual part of the brain that we can engage anywhere, at any time. For thousands of years, humanity has waged so-called religious wars and conflicts. But here, plain as day, I could see that we all use the same spiritual part of our brain. People of all different religions, people who are nonreligious and spiritual, engage the same neural correlates of spiritual perception.

And this engagement appeared to be a matter of *choice*. The same healthy young adult brain could be used for stress—for isolation, helplessness, worry, addiction, and craving—or for spiritual engagement. The same person, with the same outward life, IQ, socioeconomic status, friends, genes, family, and environment, could see a world that looked abundant and bright, or empty and insufficient. What participants saw and experienced was determined by how they marshaled their own inner life. By making a choice in perception, the same person could be either awake or strung out.

THE FMRI STUDY illuminated that we all have two modes of awareness available to us at all times: achieving awareness and awakened awareness. It's up to us which one we engage.

Achieving awareness is the perception that our purpose is to organize and control our lives. When we live through our achieving awareness, our foundational concern is *How can I get and keep what I want?* This mode of awareness is useful—and often necessary. It gives us the focused attention and commitment necessary to attain goals and enables us to direct our attention and energy into a particular task—to study for an exam, complete a project, get someplace on time, practice a skill. It allows us the focused drive and undistracted execution we need to implement and achieve our goals. It's a highly necessary and helpful form of perception.

But when overused, or exclusively used, achieving awareness overrides and changes the structure of our brains, carving pathways of depression, anxiety, stress, and craving. When out of balance, achieving awareness is narrowly focused, unguided by the bigger picture, obsessed with the same track or idea, never satisfied, and often lonely and isolated.

And it doesn't help us face undesirable outcomes. If we navigate life through our achieving awareness alone, we are often frustrated or distressed when things don't turn out as we'd planned or hoped. And even when things appear to be working out for us, we perceive that it is up to us alone to make good things happen, or prevent bad things from happening. Life is an inert stage we act upon, trying to move everyone and everything toward our individual goals and desires. This can leave us isolated, stuck in rumination, or mired in a persistent feeling of dread, stress, or even emptiness.

When we live only through our achieving awareness, we develop a perceptual problem. We have a much-inflated sense of control, even as we become disconnected from the heartbeat of everyone around us. This is a lonely, atomistic, and inherently empty way to be. Even having everything can feel like having nothing. This perception of emptiness just makes us *want more* and *try harder*—and so we're trapped in the cycle of motivation and reward. Overblown, it becomes craving and addiction: we need a bigger and bigger dose to feel good—but no amount of control or success will extinguish the craving.

When we engage our **awakened awareness**, we make use of different parts of our brain, and we literally *see more,* integrating information from multiple sources of perception. Instead of seeing ourselves as independent makers of our path, we perceive ourselves as *seekers* of our path. We look across a vast landscape and ask, *What is life showing me now?* This awakened awareness allows us to perceive more choices and opportunities available to us, feel more connected with others, understand the relationships between events in our lives, be more open to creative leaps and insights, and feel more in tune with our life's purpose and meaning.

In awakened awareness, we don't lose or forsake our goals. But we take off the blinders. We surrender our tight grip on a goal. We understand that life is a dynamic force that we can attune to and interact with. It's no longer me against the world, or me treading upon the world, but me hearing what life has to say, aware that life is meeting me where I am. I still have wishes and desires and goals, I still experience disappointment and hurt—but I lean into the flow of life, paying attention to where doors open and close.

As a result of this awakened awareness, our eyes move to meaningful events. In achieving awareness, the stranger who starts talking to us on the bus might be annoying or intrusive, or just invisible. In awakened awareness, we might hear what he says—and even see how it's relevant to our own lives. Life is no longer inert, a platform on which we try to have our needs and desires met. It's a living, conscious dialogue that includes some interesting surprises. When we engage our awakened awareness, the hard things in our lives don't go away. But we have the capacity to perceive our sorrow and struggle in a new way. Knit into the fabric of life, there is a felt knowledge that we are never really alone.

Achieving awareness is necessary. It helps us move and chase the ball up and down the field. But to decide where the ball needs to go, to see the bigger field of play, to be aware of the other players, to understand the consequences and impact of our choices—and to perceive why we are playing the game in the first place—we need our awakened awareness. In other words, our most important decisions can't be made from achieving awareness alone. We can only perceive reality accurately when we have both foundational modes of awareness on board. Every day we make thousands of choices, and we make better ones when we engage the perceptual capacity that gives us the widest, most valuable and illuminating view. We need what we learn from *both* modes of awareness to inform our actions.

We had already seen that the spiritual brain is a healthier brain. Now we could see why—we could see the neural ingredients of awakened awareness. And we could see that spiritual awakening is a choice we can make at every moment—a choice of how we perceive the world and ourselves.

CHAPTER 13

INTEGRATION IS KEY

My journeys to finding Isaiah and discovering the awakened brain had required both achieving and awakened awareness. IVF, persistence, scientific method, statistical analysis—all were necessary elements. I couldn't sit back and wait for a child or a scientific answer. Both journeys required rigorous pursuit and discerning perception. Yet achieving awareness alone didn't work. I was helped on the path by my awakened awareness. By an openness to synchronicity—the orphan on TV, the duck embryo, the grandmother and granddaughter on the subway in church clothes. By answering the call—presenting at Grand Rounds, taking a plane to Iowa. By trusting my inner knowing even when it contradicted others' plans or preferences, or even my own. A creative, dynamic interplay between achieving and awakened awareness had illuminated and clarified my path.

Integration is key. If we're using only our achieving awareness, we're caught up in what we have and don't have. We measure purpose and success by outcomes, by cravings fulfilled, by the degree to which we adhere to a preexisting plan or code. Life becomes narrow and stressful. Yet if we live only through our awakened awareness, we're untethered, full of bursts of insights but disconnected from the sphere where we might put them into action. We suffer because we're unable to made grounded decisions or discern solutions or a path forward.

We can't live exclusively in awakened awareness all the time. Elena is an American-born woman—raised right in the middle of mainstream American culture, highly educated and successful— who exited her suburban life and became a Buddhist nun, living at an isolated center where she meditated for three years, three months, three weeks, and three days. During her ordainment she experienced profound mystical experiences and a deepened spirituality—but no counseling on how to integrate back into daily life when it was time to leave the center and return home. When she ended almost forty continuous months of contemplative solitude, she became confused upon reentry. Light and sound assaulted her. Everyday conversations and transactions baffled her.

One morning she awoke at dawn in her suburban home, certain that His Holiness the Dalai Lama was calling her. She packed her suitcases, donned her saffron robe, and stood outside on the lawn, waiting for him to pick her up. The sun rose higher, noon came, then dusk, then sunset, and still she stood there, certain the Dalai Lama was on his way. In a spiritual, awakened sense, it very well may have been that she was called by the Dalai Lama to serve the world in a specific way, or more generally to deepen her practice and commitment to spiritual life. But she had been in her awakened awareness alone for so long that she could no longer discern at what level of reality this perception of spiritual calling was coming in. She thought that a literal car was about to pull up to the curb and the Dalai Lama would usher her inside.

The gift of the awakened call was lost without her achieving awareness to help her decipher and implement it effectively.

WHEN WE'RE DISINTEGRATED in either our achieving or awakened awareness, we're failing to make full use of the neural capacities that support our greatest health. But, practically speaking, how do we go about integrating our achieving and awakened awareness? What does this integration look like in our daily lives? How does it help us set goals and make decisions; be in relationship with friends, partners, families, colleagues, and communities; heal from trauma or adverse experiences; work for a better world?

Our collaborative Yale team employed an additional imaging technique, called diffusion tensor imaging (DTI), to explore the link between the brain's white matter tracts and various spiritual orientations—different stances or ways of being. DTI is essentially a measure of how well the highway is paved between regions of the brain. It works by looking at the rate and direction of water diffusion in the brain, seeing where water flows and where it trickles. Water diffuses more easily and quickly in the direction of established myelinated internal structures. By watching the path of water, you can see the brain's habitual pathways and also measure the connectivity of the brain—which parts are communicating with one another, versus remaining isolated.

We interviewed participants extensively about their lives, and they completed validated measures on their various spiritual and religious experiences, including their religious orientation, daily spiritual awareness or practices, and the role of questioning and doubt in their spiritual lives. We also measured the degree to which they engaged in a very specific construct that has been linked to long-term spiritual thriving: a way of engaging neurological and perceptual capacities in a state of quest. **Quest orientation** is characterized by a tendency to journey in life: to search for answers to meaningful personal decisions and big existential questions; to perceive doubt as positive; and to be open to change, or more accurately, open to perceiving with fresh eyes, and then using new experience to fuel change. In quest, we open ourselves to the messages from life, take seriously this discovery, and then actively use learning to shape our decisions and actions—our personal operating manual.

When we measured DTI water diffusion in the brains of twenty-four young adults, we found that a key quest attribute—openness to exploring one's religious and spiritual views—correlates with high white matter integrity in multiple tracts of the brain, including those connecting brain regions in the two hemispheres. In other words, the subjects who reported that they lived in a state of quest—with spiritual lives that included an openness to perceiving surprising answers and changing their views—had better-connected brains than those who were less open to change.

Good connection between and within brain regions signals health. It means the prefrontal cortex is connected with the parietal. The left and right hemispheres are connected. Information flows. No region is isolated from or hijacked by another—and the brain is open to present input instead of playing the same tired old record again and again. There is lively dialogue happening between thought, perception, orientation, and reflection instead of the tiresome, soupy myopia of rumination that's linked with depression, where we see the same things over and over, repeatedly reliving trauma and misery. In quest, many forms of perception and knowing are on board, all working together. The brain is able to make broad and integrated use of information coded in different ways by different regions.

Interestingly, **some of the same networks of the brain that are highly connected in quest are dysfunctionally connected in depression**. In depression, the default mode network—which processes self-relevant memories and emotionally laden reflections—becomes, in scientific parlance, internally hyperconnected and externally hypoconnected. This means that the brain focuses overly on internal, often self-referential thoughts, and disengages from the environment. Instead of receiving salient information from the world, the brain narrows, becoming self-involved and ruminative, no longer passing ideas or information on to the brain's command center to evaluate and set a course of action. When we're suffering from depression, we're not holding our perceptual catcher's mitt out to the world. We're turning it inward.

The salience network is also compromised with depression. In a healthy, questing brain, the amygdala, ventral striatum, dorsal anterior cingulate cortex, and insula work together to process affective and salient stimuli and to guide motivation and behavior. But in the depressed brain, the amygdala overruns the network and the reward circuitry breaks down. We become anxious and reactive, and are more attuned to negative stimuli. Even if there's outward information streaming in that tells us we're safe and loved and valued, we're less likely to perceive it. And when the salience network is disrupted, the brain can't pass information along to its command center. There's no regulatory voice to redirect attention to more relevant input or to revise a negative conclusion. The cognitive control network fails to get an invitation from the salience network to evaluate goals, ideas, and perceptions. And the network itself is disrupted. The lateral regions of the prefrontal cortex are less connected, making it harder to process information and regulate emotions.

In depression, parts of the brain are dysregulated and disconnected. They aren't functioning optimally or working together. But in quest, the brain is coherent and connected, its regions and networks in harmony. Essentially, **the questing brain integrates our achieving and awakened awareness**.

And when we integrate our two modes of awareness, *we literally see more*. Anna Antinori and her team at the University of Melbourne showed how openness to experience, the "big five" personality type most neurologically similar to quest, changes what we see in the world.

Antinori recruited over one hundred volunteers—some of whom measured high in openness to experience, the personality trait associated with quest and creativity—and tested them for a phenomenon called "binocular rivalry," showing them a different image in each eye and seeing how they perceived two incompatible images. When shown a green patch in one eye and a red patch in the other, most participants switched back and forth between the different images, perceiving only one color at a time. But those who were high in openness to experience had a visual perception that wasn't available to the other participants—instead of toggling between the two colors, they saw a unified red-and-green patch. They were able to see two competing stimuli simultaneously.

Our attentional networks constantly filter what sensory information comes into our conscious awareness. Our brains determine what we see and what we ignore. When we're in quest, more perceptions are available to us. The world looks fuller. We perceive a "both-and," not an "either-or." More information is streaming in, and we have more perceptual possibilities, more tools at the ready to make clear sense of it. We use our awakened awareness to pick up new information—spontaneously catching, perceiving, and valuing what streams in. And then our salience network "dings," telling us that something that could be important has landed, and we shuttle that information into our achieving awareness, where we evaluate it and decide what action to take.

Quest is a toggle between awakened and achieving awareness. We can ask a driving question through achieving awareness and then receive an answer through awakened awareness; and the opposite is also true: we can be inspired by an awakened experience and then discern its meaning and place in our lives through achieving awareness. This dynamic interplay supports innovative, creative thinking. We can problem-solve in a whole new way through quest, whether on significant personal choices, professional challenges, or the bigger lifework of disappointment, loss, and trauma. In quest, life itself becomes a creative journey full of unexpected surprises and buoyant with love, connection, and direction. We just need to choose to engage what moments of awareness we already have, take seriously our flashes of intuition or insight, and honor the ongoing interplay as it yields fresh meaning and direction. We are hardwired to awaken, transform, and expand even through trauma. If we answer the call, often with spiritual support, we can realize our great potential for an inspired life.

To be clear, there appear to be many different types of so-called depression, a broad category that captures many different symptom clusters and internal experiences. The power of the awakened brain is that it offers us a pathway through a certain type of depressive experience by encouraging us to open the door toward spiritual growth and emergence. Some forms of depression clearly benefit from medication or traditional therapy without a spiritual dimension, but neither of these classic treatments alone fulfills the promise of the "knock at the door" of a developmental depression. This sort of depression is a "call of the soul," a spiritual invitation to live more fully, love more deeply, and open into dialogue with the sacred universe. Sensed through our inner wisdom, this kind of depression—whether it occurs at a ripe life stage such as adolescence or midlife, or in response to struggle or trauma—beckons us into a lifetime of awakening.

The more we practice the toggle between achieving and awakened awareness, the more we tune into an inspired way of thinking, feeling, and walking in the world. Our lives become full not only of solutions but also of wonder as we discover our own sacred journey, and how our individual journey dovetails with others' journeys and with life itself. Most important of all, quest is not just for the accomplished and enlightened few, for monks and clergy and spiritual teachers. Quest is available to each one of us. It's how we're built to live.

MY SCIENTIFIC CAREER began as a journey to understand the protective benefits of spirituality—to discover how spirituality buffers us against depression, anxiety, and substance abuse, and how spirituality lives in the brain. When we lifted the hood, we discovered three key ways to bring the wisdom of our awakened brain into our daily lives: through **awakened attention, awakened connection,** and **awakened heart**. In the next chapters I'll share stories and practices to help us cultivate these core dimensions of spirituality, increasing our brain's health and enabling us to lead lives that are effective, connected, and inspired.

CHAPTER 14

AWAKENED ATTENTION

I love to kayak on the Saugatuck River, a few miles downstream from home. One afternoon I was on the river alone, moving fast, headed straight down the middle of the water, when a flock of geese swam toward me, honking at top volume, craning their necks at the right-hand riverbank. *"Er-ah! Er-ah!"* they screeched. If I'd stayed in my achieving awareness and stuck to my goal-oriented, top-down attention, I would have ignored the loud geese—even thought them annoying—and kept going full-speed down the middle of the river. But instead I noticed their call and followed the deliberate direction of their necks. I paddled hard right, narrowly missing a huge cement block submerged just under the surface, a remnant of an old bridge that would have capsized my kayak, or worse, if I'd hit it. In achieving awareness alone, animals are barely sentient. In awakened awareness, they appear as alert guides.

When we're driven by achieving awareness alone, we're more likely to be limited by self-obsession and craving, and less sensitive to the field of life around us. Through awakened attention, we open up more channels of perception. We learn not only to notice but also to draw meaning from what shows up in our lives. We see more, and we're better able to use what we see.

TO ENGAGE OUR innate capacity for awakened attention, we first quiet the "little me," turning down our achieving awareness so that our awakened awareness can emerge. There are many conscious ways to do this—through chanting, prayer, creative expression, meditation, and more.

One way into awakened attention is to start through mindfulness practice, and a large body of scientific research examines the neuroanatomy of mindfulness. When we intentionally detach from the tight grip of our thoughts, two important things happen in our brains: we activate the dorsolateral prefrontal cortex and anterior cingulate cortex; and we deactivate the posterior cingulate cortex, which is the start of the default mode network. In other words, mindfulness helps us turn up command control at the front of the brain, focusing and strengthening our attention, and turn down the default mode network, quieting the negative hold of runaway thoughts. We turn down the ruminative racket, readying our awareness for fresh insights.

Mindfulness has been shown to decrease our emotional reactivity, rectify distorted views of the self, and loosen the hold of addiction. In one study, people interested in quitting smoking used mindfulness practice to detach from feelings of craving. Mindfulness, as attentional control, didn't make the craving go away, but it interrupted the loop of habit, allowing participants to experience craving and still change their behavior, choosing not to light up a cigarette. By interrupting and quieting obsessive thoughts—turning up the dorsolateral prefrontal cortex and anterior cingulate cortex, and turning down the posterior cingulate cortex—mindfulness takes us to the doorway of a new perceptual capacity.

The same is true of spending time in nature. Gregory Bratman, an ecologist at the University of Washington, has investigated how the environment influences human well-being. Concerned about the link between increased urbanization and increased rates of mental illness, he wanted to measure the emotional and cognitive impact of exposure to nature, and examined the effects of a fifty-minute walk in nature and a fifty-minute walk in an urban environment. He found that the walk in nature had significant, measurable benefits: decreased anxiety, rumination, and negative affect; preservation of positive affect; and increased working memory performance. In another study, this time investigating the effects of a ninety-minute walk in nature versus an urban setting, he found that along with a decrease in self-reported rumination, the nature-walk participants showed decreased activity in the subgenual prefrontal cortex, quieting thoughts and inner chatter.

Mindfulness and exposure to nature, as examples of "quieting" practice, prep our brains for spiritual awareness. In other words, quieting the racket makes more possible, it brings us to the front door. Now at the threshold, we have the option to take another step. We can choose to practice awakened attention.

ONE POWERFUL WAY to engage our awakened attention is through noticing synchronicity in our daily lives. Social justice leader and theologian Reverend Walter Earl Fluker's experience powerfully illustrates the golden thread of synchronicity running through his life.

He grew up on the South Side of Chicago, where his sharecropper parents had landed when they left Mississippi in their forties. His father had a fourth-grade education; his mother couldn't write her own name. The streets were an especially dangerous place for Walter, a skinny, bookish kid. Yet over and over, guides, as he calls them, were posted for him.

The first was Mrs. Watley, an elderly neighbor whose husband worked at a printing company. She stopped Walter on his way home from school one day and gave him paper and a set of sharpened pencils that smelled of clean wood. He went home and sat at the kitchen table and started writing—his first memory of writing poetry.

Then there was his teacher Mrs. Alice McClaskey, who came into his life at a time of struggle, when he was bored at vocational high school; worried for his parents, who'd been robbed several times in the middle of the street; and scared for his older brother, who'd been drafted into the military and sent to Vietnam. Mrs. McClaskey introduced him to literature, in particular Shakespeare, and, as Walter says, "created a space for me to be me." When she passed away during his senior year, he wrote a poem for her and was asked to deliver it at the high school memorial service, where another guide, Mrs. Adelaide Ward, observed his interest in poetry and writing, and arranged an internship for him at an all-white industrial advertising agency downtown.

Then he was drafted. Even without a college education, he managed to secure a position as a post chaplain's clerk at Fort Riley, Kansas. One of his tasks was to help prepare a bulletin each Sunday on old lithograph paper. The chaplain often included meditations from someone named Howard Thurman— a man he didn't hear or think of again for years, not until he was in seminary in Illinois, grieving a divorce and trying to gain the attention of the beautiful woman who lived in the apartment next door. After he spent two years knocking on her door, making every excuse he could think of to get her to notice him, she finally invited him into her apartment, and there on the wall was a huge poster that said *As long as a man has a dream in his heart, he cannot lose the significance of living*. It was autographed by Howard Thurman.

When Walter and Sharon began dating, Howard Thurman was invited to the seminary where Walter was studying, and Walter was chosen as the student escort to pick up Thurman from the airport. Sharon prepared a lunch for them to share, and Walter discovered that she was Thurman's goddaughter. Thurman looked at Walter with probing eyes and said, "Well, who are you? What are you trying to do with your life?" Later, Sharon brought Walter to Atlanta to meet her parents, and Howard and his wife, Sue Bailey Thurman, joined them one evening. So began an important mentorship.

In his final year of seminary, Walter was still trying to work out his calling. Should he finish seminary or go to law school? What was he meant to do? He kept begging for a revelation, but none came. Desperate for guidance, he wrote Thurman a letter. Thurman's handwritten response arrived, covered in doodles: *You're like a little boy under the Christmas tree who has so many gifts he doesn't know which one to open first. The main thing is, you must wait and listen for the sound of the genuine which is within you. When you hear it, that will be your voice, and that will be the voice of God.*

"The ground shifted when I read that," Walter said. "I had no idea what it all meant—but I knew it was right."

With his application rejected from a graduate program at Northwestern, where Sharon was working on her doctorate, Walter began a PhD at Boston University. He woke up one April morning hearing Thurman's laughter, and wrote him a letter, thanking him for all he had done to set him on his path. A week later, Sharon visited him in Boston. They were sitting on the steps of the Episcopal Divinity School in Cambridge when a colleague approached them and said, "Howard Thurman died this morning."

Most of Thurman's collected works and papers later found a permanent home at Boston University, and Walter, still working on his doctorate, decided to devote his dissertation to the concepts of community developed by Howard Thurman and Martin Luther King, Jr. Later, as the editor of the Howard Thurman Papers, Walter assigned researchers to read and organize Thurman's entire life's work, and thus Thurman continued to guide his intellectual and professional life for the next forty years.

"Guides and synchronicities are not things we look for," Walter said. "We're visited by them. When we're open, we experience them."

Even obstacles often appear at just the right time to teach us something important. I created this exercise called Three Doors to help show that when we're using the lens of achieving awareness alone, we see boulders blocking our path, but when we engage our awakened attention, the boulders are actually stepping-stones that show us the path forward. To build awakened attention, I have developed this practice, which I've shared with bankers and lawyers, U.S. Army generals, Columbia students, homeless youth in New York City, and patients working through suffering and building well-being. The exercise is equally relevant and effective for everyone, because it calls our attention to the road of life.

1. On a sheet of paper or in your journal, draw the road of your life.
2. Identify a place on the road where you faced a hurdle: a loss, a disappointment, a death; a time when the thing you

wanted—a job, a relationship, an award or accomplishment, an acceptance letter from a particular school—seemed lined up, in reach; and then somehow, unexpectedly, the door slammed, and you didn't get what you wanted or what you thought you were going to get. Draw the slammed door on the road.

3. Now consider what happened as a result of that loss or disappointment that wouldn't have happened otherwise. Because the door closed, and because you didn't claw ahead trying to force it back open, because you stopped and looked around, you saw a new door you hadn't noticed before. What new insight or connection or path emerged, what new doorway opened, when the first door closed? Add the open door, leading to the new landscape along the road.

4. Next, can you locate a messenger or helper who showed up and, with or without knowing they played a role, somehow supported or guided you? Perhaps it was someone you'd never met before or someone you knew well; someone who showed up in person or called you or sent you a letter, or someone you thought of at a crucial moment. Who were the messengers or helpers who pointed you to the open door? Draw the messenger(s) on the road.

5. Repeat steps 2 through 4 twice more, so that your road of life shows three doors that closed and three that opened, and who showed up along the way to point you on your path.

The exercise helps us identify three concrete examples of times when our ventral attention network afforded us new vision. And when we observe how doors have closed and opened in our lives, and notice who showed up on our path, we are better able to see that loss and disappointment are often experiences that deepen, not threaten, our lives.

As Walter Earl Fluker said, "Sometimes when we're not open to guidance, guides still show up. And if we're stubborn, they have a way of letting us know."

Ultimately, he says, synchronistic experiences are "moments of ecstasy when I'm most myself."

The more we open to the guidance of synchronicities, the better we can engage life as a creative act, living in a way that allows life to reveal itself.

WHEN WE AWAKEN our ventral attention network, we broaden not only what we see but also our perception of what counts as real, life-changing information.

Major General Thomas Solhjem, the head of the U.S. Army Chaplain Corps, explains that his deliberate use of awakened attention helps him keep what he calls his "divine appointments."

"Where you're supposed to be isn't always where the mission says you should be," he says.

Once, when he served in the Rangers, there was a big operation under way, and, pragmatically speaking, he should have chosen to be with B Company, where there were more people. But he used awakened attention to guide his decision, praying for direction, asking, "Where do you need me to be?" Through quieting his achieving awareness and engaging awakened awareness, he felt a strong conviction that he needed to be with one of the helicopters that was bringing people out.

And so he was right there when small arms fire on the ground hit the helo and the crew chief was shot in the head. They moved the crew chief and three other injured Rangers to a small fixed-wing aircraft with full surgical capability. Solhjem held the head of the crew chief while the doctor tried to piece him back together. Finally the doctor turned to Solhjem and said, "Chaplain, I've done everything I can now. The rest is up to you."

"So we prayed on that aircraft for those four souls," Solhjem says. "All of them survived. If I'd gone someplace else during the operation, I would have missed that divine appointment."

Solhjem explains that when he senses guidance through awakened attention, he doesn't "get an audible from outer space." Rather, "there's an inner sense. It's listening to yourself, listening to what's being fed to you that propels you in the right direction. It's more than mission planning."

He adds, "When I'm directed by the need for something outside myself, or the need for something within myself to be connected; when I'm attentive to the reality that I could miss if I'm not paying attention—then I get the best spiritual outcomes and life is the richest in its reward. And you realize you didn't get there alone."

Now he works in the Pentagon as the principal religious and spiritual adviser to senior Army leadership. While traveling around the globe and reaching out to provide spiritual leadership to the Army family, he makes sure to build "walking around" time into his calendar—time to move through the world's largest office building, trusting that he'll run into someone he's supposed to run into and a conversation will start. Whether he's in the E-ring or the latrine, or at some remote camp, post, or station, he's likely to encounter a person who, in response to his "How are you doing? How are you *really* doing? How's your soul?" might say "I'm struggling a little with my teenager," or "My husband's ill." Through an intentional practice of awakened attention, he keeps his divine appointments with a sense of anticipation and expectation of some greater purpose.

. . .

TWENTIETH-CENTURY VIEWS of the mind describe imagination as something we construct. Imagination is invention. Make-believe. But in awakened awareness, imagination is not an act of creation so much as an act of perception—a way of detecting information. Just as we detect heat from a burner when our hand gets too close to the stove, so we detect images—whether visual, auditory, or through any of our senses—that allow us to perceive something real. When we engage in guided imaging, we can perceive information that is highly therapeutic, useful, or directive.

Visualizations can invite people, or a sacred presence, or fellow living beings into our awareness. I've seen wonderful, healing shifts happen for people using visualizations of people in their lives with whom they had reached an impasse, including those living and deceased. And in terms of self-discovery, I've seen powerful personal realization come through this simple, age-old visualization:

> Close your eyes and use long, steady breathing to quiet your achieving awareness.
>
> Clear out your inner space. Then, invite an animal, and watch to see who comes. Ask, "What say you?"

This animal visualization gave important and healing information to Darren, a young actor who was in recovery after years of addiction. The animal that popped into his awareness was a chameleon. At first, this upset him. "A chameleon," he said. "That's me. Always playing a role. Trying to be what others want me to be." He could only see the chameleon through his achieving lens—his battle with addiction, unworthiness, and emptiness. His self-critical perception took over. "I'm always just putting on shows," he said. "I'm just a front, with nothing inside."

But then he heard how hard he was being on himself. Seeing the chameleon, and observing his reaction to it, brought him to a fresh realization, helping him see his habit of self-criticism. He consciously dropped his achieving lens and asked, "What if I accept the chameleon, the one animal in the world that came to me?"

When he gave himself permission to embrace the image of the chameleon instead of judging it, he saw something new. A chameleon is very adaptable. It's quick and quick-witted, and knows how to survive in all sorts of environments. In a flash of insight, he shed the old perception that he was a poser and a pleaser, and perceived himself and his strengths in a new way: creative, nimble.

When our ventral attention network is engaged, we are open to noticing and making meaning in ways that support our growth and healing. Sometimes the information and images we receive are confusing—even uncomfortable.

Reverend Walter Earl Fluker was in a therapy session when a bizarre image came to him: a huge mother opossum with baby opossums hanging off her back. It was so unexpected that he burst out laughing. During the session, he also had the sensation of holding many children, and felt overwhelmed and afraid he would drop them. Then an impression of a memory rose, the feeling of being dropped as a young child. He knew his mother had had epileptic seizures, so this old sensory impression, this long-forgotten memory of being dropped, instantly made sense to him.

It was also frightening. He was a child of the academy, supposed to be concerned only with tight epistemological structures and quantifiable truth. This information, though it squared with some of the known facts of his life, was coming to him in such an unquantifiable way.

The memory was painful, too. It was terrifying to feel the secure arms release him, his body falling away. Still, as he reexperienced the fall, there was a sense beyond the fear, not a voice exactly, but a presence around him that said, not in words but in feeling, *Don't worry. We'll hold you.* It gave him a great and inexplicable peace.

A week later, he traveled to Buffalo for work, and he brought his two young sons with him, taking them to the Buffalo Museum of Science on his morning off. They rounded a corner in the museum and stumbled on an exhibit of a mother opossum, little baby possums hanging off her coat, just like the image that had come out of nowhere in therapy. His hands shook as he and his sons read that opossums are marsupials, that they carry their babies in a pouch, incubating their young until they are strong enough to climb out of the pouch, cling to the mother's coat, and finally stand on their own.

As Reverend Fluker took some breaths to steady himself, the meaning of the opossum came to him through his achieving and awakened awareness, through his head and his heart. Professionally, he was in the process of designing a model for ethical leadership, striving to find or create a source of protection and nourishment for emerging leaders—young men and women who had come from the places where he grew up. The opossum instantly inspired the idea of a moral incubator—a way to keep young leaders physically safe, mentally disciplined, intellectually astute, psychologically and spiritually whole, and morally anchored as they learned to lead. Emotionally, the opossum brought the sense of the presence that told him, *You are held. Don't be afraid.*

"We're isolated and alienated," he said. "We feel lonely most of the time, we're so afraid—because we lack the knowledge that we're held."

WHEN WE AWAKEN our attention, we can access the perceptions that help us rewrite our understanding of the world. Major General Solhjem introduced me to a number of U.S. military chaplains who use awakened attention to help the people in their care. This is how they describe the healing process they use:

1. Tell a detailed narrative of the traumatic incident. In memory, go to the space and place of the trauma. Relive it, engaging sensory memories—sights, smells, sounds, etc.
2. During the telling, at the moment of greatest grief or regret, express the feelings of remorse or responsibility.
3. Then invite your higher power in—whatever image of transcendence resonates for you. This can include personal prayer, a circle of prayer, or in some traditions a laying-on of hands.
4. See what fresh rearrangement of meaning spontaneously comes.
5. Then return to the narrative with that new information.

A senior chaplain shared with me the story of a man who had been stuck in a state of trauma for ten years, ever since he accidentally shot and killed a fellow American soldier, a member of his squad. He had become numb and cut off, inaccessible to his family, and so consumed by guilt that he had grown meticulously obsessive; so afraid of making a devastating mistake that he could barely function. For years, his treatment had focused on helping him disrupt the obsessive thoughts and behaviors. But it wasn't working, probably because his obsessive tendencies were his way of protecting himself against his terrible feelings of guilt and unworthiness. Recognizing that this x-axis treatment model wasn't working, the chaplain brought in the y-axis. He engaged the man in quest.

First, he asked the soldier to tell the story of the painful incident, to relive the trauma.

"I'm on base," the soldier began. "I've just cleaned and reloaded my gun. I hear a noise and I swivel. And the gun goes off. My friend is on the ground. There's blood everywhere."

"What are you feeling?" the chaplain asked.

"Awful. Guilty. Scared. I'm screaming and it's the worst pain I've ever felt. My body feels paralyzed."

"Let's invite God into this moment," the chaplain said. Straddling two time zones—the present moment, and the moment of trauma the soldier was reliving—the chaplain offered a prayer, reaching out to God for guidance. The two men prayed together.

Suddenly, tears washed over the soldier's cheeks. "I heard God," he said. "I looked at the gun and saw that the safety was off. And God told me, 'You've made a horrible mistake. You didn't do this intentionally. You are forgiven. Everyone is forgiven.'"

A common misunderstanding in the mental health field is that it's the traumatic or painful event that makes us depressed. But mental suffering isn't so much the direct result of trauma as it is an outcome of how trauma takes hold in our daily experience of life, how it narrows and limits our perception. Healing doesn't happen through revisiting the trauma, as Esther Klein had been forced to do on Unit 6, but by bringing new insight and information to bear on the trauma—by illuminating the truth that has been obscured.

Plenty of times, others had tried to convince the soldier he was guiltless. But he hadn't been able to detach from a feeling of total, definitive unworthiness. In going back to the intransigent moment, the event that had trapped his life at an impasse, and opening up to spiritual awareness, fresh information had tumbled in, allowing for a rearrangement of meaning. His epiphany came in the spiritual language he knew, but it could have come in a different image, as in the spiritual narratives generated by the subjects in our first fMRI study at Yale—the sound of voices singing together, the sunlight shining through trees, a grandmother's comforting smell as expressions of ultimate sacredness or goodness. In his case, it was the direct voice of God offering forgiveness. He no longer believed that he was evil, wrong, morally culpable forever. He was able to move forward with a deep inner knowing that he was worthy of forgiveness.

The chaplain shared a second story of healing and transformation through awakened attention. A woman who had been assaulted several years earlier had coped with the trauma by putting up very hard boundaries with men. She had foreclosed on ever again having intimacy in her life, because she found it impossible to trust others—and because she felt ashamed, thinking that the assault was somehow her fault. As she told her story—the date at a restaurant, the walk home, the drink, the bedroom, the assault by a man she liked and trusted—the chaplain, using their shared spiritual language, encouraged her to open up awakened awareness by offering a prayer for her healing and restoration.

"Let God into the bedroom," he said. "What do you see?"

"I see an innocent girl," she said. "She's hurt. God says, 'It's not your fault.'"

Awakened awareness opened up the possibility for renewal—

a big shake-up of meaning, an upheaval of the old broken record of blame and shame, and the opening chords of a new song: *I was hurt and it's not my fault. I don't have to push people away.*

WHEN I THINK of awakened attention, I think of the iconic painting on the ceiling of the Sistine Chapel of God giving life to Adam. So are we given life, by consciousness. Through awakened attention, we're available for surprise, for new information that turns our head. When new awareness comes, it's like the hand of life reaching out to touch our hand. We're not just a tiny, atomistic self alone in the unfathomable universe. We're not alone. Life is always reaching out to us. And through integrated awareness, we're available to see, feel, and know life's hand, and to reach back—to be in constant dialogue with the consciousness that runs in, through, and around us, at once a part of life and contributing to it. When we awaken this capacity, we grow and heal.

CHAPTER 15

AWAKENED CONNECTION

A few months after the *inipi,* in July 2001, an attendant ushered Phil and me through a sunny playroom in Babies
House #5 in St. Petersburg, toward a large crib where five babies
lay on their stomachs in a circle with a few toys—a bright blue
ball, a striped wooden block, a painted wooden animal—at the
center. One of the baby girls in the circle began to cry. A round-
cheeked baby boy pushed the ball toward her, and watched her
expectantly. When she pawed at the ball with interest, he smiled
and cooed gleefully. The baby boy was Isaiah. Our son.

"The babies comfort each other," the attendant told us.
"When one is crying, the other children cheer them up by passing toys."

I held my son for the first time. His warm weight filled my
arms. I buried my nose in his fine blond hair, I kissed his tummy,
his delicious round cheeks. I inhaled his fresh baby smell, held
him to my heart. He pressed his chubby hands against my chest
and arched his back so he could gaze at me. Then he touched my
face. I'd never felt such a consuming surge of love and recogni-

tion. I could barely let go to hand him to Phil. Then I sat transfixed by son and father. Tears slid down Phil's cheeks.

Our adoption guide shared knowledge of two letters that our son's biological mother had left at the hospital one week after his birth. The first said, *I'll be back in six months for little Vladislav. I need to earn enough money.* The second waived parental rights and said, *Please, be sure our little Vladislav is loved.* Here we were to love him, the answer to his mother's request. And Isaiah the answer to ours.

We'd been warned that Russia enforced a law of detainment—a mandatory waiting period for all international adoptions. We were expected to meet our son and then go back home without him. I understood the reasons for the law—to be sure that the adopting family is safe before a child is united with them in a new country. In the abstract, the waiting period made sense. But every day he wasn't home with us was a day we were scared of losing him. We were already a family. We were brimming with love. Isaiah had already spent ten months in an orphanage. Why delay a minute longer? Practically speaking, it seemed unwise. I wanted time to bond with Isaiah before his newborn sibling arrived. And as the months passed and my due date approached, it would only be harder to travel.

We requested a court date to plead our case, but the judge who typically presided over these matters was leaving on vacation the next day. No one would be available for a hearing. Our adoption agency made countless phone calls, trying to figure out if a court in a different city could make a ruling on the case, and had just about tapped out all the options when a call came to us at our hotel. The original judge's daughter had won a science prize, and the family vacation had been canceled so that they could be in town for the award ceremony. The judge would hear our case in the morning.

I stood before her in the muggy courtroom the next day, wearing a loose dress to cut the heat and accommodate the gentle swell of my belly.

"Your Honor, we're requesting that you please waive the law of detainment. We want to take home our spiritual child."

The judge looked at us sternly. For a terrible moment I thought she might ask me about my pregnancy, refuse to let us adopt with a biological child on the way. But then I saw that her face was taut because she was holding back tears.

"Children need to be loved," she said, and, with a stroke of her gavel, waived the law.

WHEN WE ARRIVED home with Isaiah, we immediately sat him down by the Saugatuck River. He took it all in: the light on the water, the thick trees in full leaf, all that green and sky and birdsong. In ten months of life, he had been outside the orphanage only once, when he was rushed to a hospital for a tear duct operation. With twenty babies under the care of one or two women, it wasn't practical or possible to get the little ones out in the air or the sun. And so he'd never seen trees or the open sky. He rubbed his bare feet in the soft grass. His eyes shone and he reached for us, as though to call our attention to the wonder, to share it with us. It's a moment I'll never forget.

From the day we'd seen the orphan on TV, the story had been teaching us: love begets love. Isaiah's first week home, our neighbors hosted a welcome party at a playground near an old white clapboard New England church. They brought heaps of food and gifts and notes of support and advice—all the things they wished they'd known when they became parents. We were moved and surprised by the huge outpouring of warmth and connection that welcomed us into the realm of family.

Now, when I visited the OB for a checkup or ultrasound, Isaiah was by my side, in his stroller. The baby within me was active, kicking. Isaiah looked at me, babbling, and pumped his legs. The kicks within me and beside me matched.

I was still learning not to hold my breath every minute of the pregnancy. But the pathway of this conception made the pregnancy feel sure and strong. Isaiah's arrival and all that I had experienced leading up to finding him had changed me. I knew I could stiffen up, afraid to surrender control; or I could allow the world to guide and unfold.

When I went into labor, my mom drove fast from Boston to be with Isaiah while he slept. I felt encircled by love, completely supported and held. But during labor, as the relentless pain mounted, as hours and hours passed and the labor failed to progress and the baby failed to come, fear swallowed me. I thought my body would break. I could see terror in Phil's face.

Finally, the doctor said, "It's cephalopelvic disproportion. There's no way this baby is going to fit through your body frame. We're going to prep you for surgery."

Phil had once told me that he was afraid that I would die in childbirth. He clenched my hand as the nurse wheeled me to the operating room. It was disorienting to see his face obscured by a mask, to see the curtains drawn across my body, separating me from myself. My lower body felt numb. Then I heard a baby cry.

"She's here!" Phil said.

Before I knew it, they had cut the umbilical cord and bathed the baby, and the nurse held her up, her body curved from toe to head, a ridge of fluffy, thick, jet-black hair standing straight up from her crown. Leah. My first impression: that my daughter must be powerful to have hair like that. The nurse placed her tenderly on my chest, right over my heart, her warmth and dearness seeping into me.

A few hours later, Leah and I lay in bed in the hospital room. Phil had gone home to sleep for a few hours and to be with Isaiah when he woke. I was alone with her. I gazed at her—the pure innocence, the wise, celestial quality that made her seem eight hundred years old. Like all newborn babies, she seemed at once ancient and brand-new. I smiled at this little being with her age-old face.

"I love you," I whispered.

She opened her eyes. She wobbled her head to face mine. In the night she seemed to grin at me, and wink one tiny wise eye.

The next morning, Phil brought Isaiah to the hospital to meet his newborn sister.

"Baby, baby!" he cried, reaching for her.

Just someone who can love, I'd said in the adoption agency all those months ago.

Leah closed her tiny fist around his finger. She looked at her brother as if they had been reunited.

I was struck again by the unlikely journey and joining together of our family. I thought of the quantum physics research on entanglement—the relationship between particles so intimately linked that a change to one affects the other, even when they are separated at a distance. If entanglement happens between the smallest increments of matter, could it also occur between living beings? Between a woman sitting tongue-tied in a smoky tent in South Dakota, and a baby waking up in an orphanage in Russia? Between Isaiah and Leah, spiritual twins conceived half a globe apart but connected from the beginning?

I also thought of a continuing education symposium I'd attended at Harvard Medical School a year or two before Isaiah came. Dr. Larry Dossey, a longtime medical doctor in Dallas—a strapping, commanding man in his sixties who looked like he'd once played quarterback on his high school football team—had given a presentation on the power of prayer and intuition in medicine, a surprising and welcome topic at a rigorous, mainstream medical school. He likened the sorts of intuition he'd witnessed in medical contexts to the peculiar bond he shared with his twin brother—a "twin thing" many identical twin pairs experience, a way of knowing, or even sharing, what the other twin is going through, even when they are physically apart. The same thought or feeling or physical sensation seemed to happen simultaneously in two different brains or bodies. "As practitioners," Dr. Dossey said, "we cannot ignore the nonlocality of consciousness." He went on to explain that our consciousness is actually part of one field of consciousness that he calls One Mind.

Hands shot up all over the auditorium, people clambering to ask some version of the same question: *How does it work?*

He smiled. "In the medical field," he said, "we often know *that* something works before we have a clue about *how* it works." Many medications—aspirin, penicillin, general anesthetics—were found to be effective treatments for inflammation, pain, or infection before we could explain the mechanism by which they were effective. "And you know," he added, chuckling, "I've never seen a patient who needed major surgery refuse a general anesthetic because the anesthesiologist couldn't explain precisely how it works."

I felt the same way about the *inipi*. My inability to explain what had happened didn't obscure my absolute joy and wonder in the imminent arrival of two children. Dr. Dossey's words ran through my mind. *The nonlocality of consciousness.* Paired with what we understood about quantum entanglement, nonlocal consciousness suggested that just as tiny particles can become bonded and interconnected, so can minds or awarenesses. Perhaps nonlocal consciousness was what I'd felt in the *inipi,* that sense of collective focus and awareness shared by the women in the tent, and also the connection with a larger source that the healer had helped us tap into. It seemed especially significant that the child who had come wasn't a daughter, as Phil had said he wanted, but a son. The women in the *inipi* had prayed for healing for their lost, missing, and suffering sons, and life had sent us *our* missing son. He hadn't materialized like food ordered from a takeout menu. He'd come through dialogue and connection with others and the universe. What was the mechanism of this connection?

BEGINNING IN 1987, Dr. Jacobo Grinberg, a neuropsychologist at the University of Mexico, ran a series of experiments that began the same way: Two people would sit in a room together and meditate for twenty minutes, intentionally focusing on establishing a strong bond. Then they were sent to separate, electromagnetically shielded rooms where Grinberg took different measurements of their brain activity. For example, he examined EEG readouts and found that after the participants had intentionally bonded, their brain-wave patterns would begin to sync up even though they were in separate rooms with no way to communicate. In another version of the experiment, once the meditators were in separate, shielded rooms, the lab tech flashed a bright light in one participant's eyes. The one hundred random flashes of light were visible on the EEG readout as sudden spikes or shocks.

Fascinatingly, when Grinberg compared the two EEGs—one from the participant who had been exposed to the flashes of light and one from the participant in the separate, shielded room—he discovered that the brain-wave shocks correlated 25 percent of the time. The participant who had not been exposed to the flashes of light still *mentally* registered a quarter of the time the flashes that were *physically* registered by the other participant. It appeared that the electrical activity of one brain was passing simultaneously into the other brain with no electrical connection or conventional signal being passed between the two. The overlap was much too significant to be explained merely by chance. By what mechanism was information being shared between the two brains? It was as though the two brains were in some way one brain—simultaneously separate and united.

"Entrainment" is the term for when two oscillations become synchronized—like when two tuning forks come to vibrate at the same frequency or two pendulums begin to synchronize and swing at the same tempo. Jacobo Grinberg's research had revealed brain-wave entrainment among empathically bonded pairs. Andrew Newberg, a neuroscientist and director of research at the Marcus Institute of Integrative Health in Philadelphia, found, through MRI and PET scans, that the strength of entrainment mounts when we add more people together in a transcendent state. People who pray together, in this case actually in the same room, accelerate the rate at which fellow worshippers activate neuropathways of a prayerful state. And it's as though the spiritual state is not only shared but also contagious. If nine people are praying together, their brains are entrained, and when a tenth person enters the room, the newcomer quickly arrives at the same entrained, spiritual state. (Perhaps this dovetails with the Jewish law of a minyan, requiring that ten worshippers must be present to conduct a religious service.)

Numerous EEG studies have shown that when two people are emotionally in sync, mirroring each other on a task, or emotionally connected in an empathic state, their two brains become synchronized. Oscillating brain waves synchronize to be in the same phase (the waves go up and down together), and this is particularly true for the wavelength called alpha (8–12 Hz). Remarkably, alpha synchronization is coming from the region of the parietal, the same posterior brain region where we saw cortical thickening in the Columbia MRI study of spiritual adults overcoming depression, and fMRI activity in the Yale study of live-action spiritual experience. Picking up on alpha is the wave we ride to unified awareness—to awakened connection.

How does brain entrainment happen, and what are the benefits of this kind of connection?

A fascinating study led by Pavel Goldstein at the University of Haifa sought to investigate brain-to-brain coupling—or resonance—as a possible mechanism for alleviating pain. The scientific community already recognized that when we experience empathy for someone in pain, we engage the same brain structures as the person in pain. In other words, pain and empathy for pain activate the same neural networks—specifically, the bilateral anterior insula and anterior mid-cingulate cortex. If brain mirroring is an essential neural component of empathy, Goldstein and his team reasoned, might it also underlie our capacity to heal and alleviate pain?

Using a technique called hyperscanning, which allows researchers to simultaneously monitor the brain activity of at least two people as they engage in a mutual exchange, Goldstein's team watched what happened in the brains of male-female romantic partners as they held hands and comforted each other through pain. For consistency's sake, and because women have been shown to benefit from social support more than men, the women were assigned the "target" role, and the men the "comforter" role. The couples were tested as they held hands, sat together with no physical contact, or sat in separate rooms, during pain and no-pain conditions. Scanners recorded the neural activity of both partners throughout the experiment so that the team could explore two questions: first, whether caring touch increases brain-to-brain synchrony and, second, whether there was any correlation between the degree of brain-to-brain synchrony and the success of the comforter in alleviating his partner's pain. Taken together, the study explored whether brain-to-brain resonance might be a factor in love's healing power.

Goldstein and his team found that there were two significant outcomes of handholding during the pain condition: interpersonal touch increased the comforter's empathic accuracy and decreased the target's experience of pain. In other words, healing touch enhances both our capacity to comfort and our success in alleviating a loved one's pain. Also, a specific network of brain resonance seems to play a role. During the pain-touch condition, the scanners revealed a strong mirroring or synchrony between mainly the parietal region of the women's brains and the right occipital, temporal, and parietal regions of the men's brains. It seemed that they had found the two-brain circuitry of the caring embrace, the soothing and reassuring coming together in a comforting "There, there." This interbrain synchrony is primarily in the alpha wavelength. It appears that our shared synchronization of alpha becomes more and more in phase based upon the intensity of close presence or touch, the level of pain or need for comfort, and the felt intimacy of the couple. Who are we to each other? We are built to comfort each other.

Goldstein and team offered two possible explanations for the finding. First, that social touch communicates social understanding, which in turn activates the reward circuitry in the brain, thus decreasing pain. And, that interpersonal touch alleviates pain by blurring the borders between self and other, creating a state of unitive love that helps the comforter both "feel" the target's pain and transmit care and support. Both ways, this study shows that when we feel empathy and transmit caring and comfort, our brains become coupled. They share oneness. And this oneness is a vital mechanism or condition of healing.

In another innovative study, Dr. Jeanne Achterberg showed that love's healing power might be transmitted not only through touch or physical proximity but also remotely. At the North Hawaii Community Hospital in Waimea, Achterberg used fMRI technology to examine whether healing thoughts sent at a distance might correlate with activation of certain brain functions in the subjects receiving the healing intentions. Experienced indigenous Hawaiian healers each selected a person with whom they felt a compassionate bond, and these receivers were placed in a scanner and isolated from all forms of sensory contact from the healer. The healers entered a scanner in a different building and were monitored as they sent healing intentions to their subjects at randomly selected two-minute intervals. The receivers had no way to anticipate or discern with their senses when the healing messages were being sent. And yet, ten times out of eleven, at the exact time the healer sent the intention, specific areas of the patients' brains—precise locations in the anterior and middle cingulate, precuneus, and frontal regions—activated. The probability that this would happen by chance alone is less than one in ten thousand. Achterberg drew the conclusion that it's possible for compassionate healing intentions sent at a distance to have a direct physical effect on the recipient—that when we are bonded, we can influence one another's bodies and mental processes.

A SYNCHRONISTIC EXPERIENCE on a lecture tour reinforced this perception. In Provo, Utah, giving an academic talk on spirituality as a resilience factor, I was jolted by the starry, piercing gazes of an older man and woman sitting in the very back row of the 400-seat auditorium. They followed my talk with such radiant attention, it was as though they were beaming lights at me. The sunny blast of their gaze seemed to penetrate me physically, a pleasant warmth gathering in my chest. They sat shoulder to shoulder, leaning into each other with exquisite presence and connection. In a sea of people, they stood out. Across the vast, dark room, their eyes sparkled with love.

I had to meet them. After the talk, I raced up the aisle. They seemed to sense I was headed toward them and waited for me, then warmly shook my hand. Dr. Gary Weaver had dark hair and clear blue eyes, his squarish build tidily tucked into a crisp collared shirt. His wife, Colleen, wore a long skirt and rich brown cowboy boots, her light hair dusting the shoulders of her colorful blouse. They thanked me for the talk, saying that the themes of spirituality and resiliency resonated with their work.

I was due at a small, invitation-only academic lunch at the university faculty club, but didn't want to leave without knowing more about the Weavers. I sensed they had something important to teach me, and so on a whim I asked my hosts to squeeze them in at my table.

Gary and Colleen told me that for thirty years, they had worked with kids who'd survived horrible abuse and then become abusers, who'd already sat before a judge three or more times and were going to be transferred from juvenile detention to adult prison if they blew their last shot. The Weavers were their last chance. And I later learned they had an 85 percent success rate in their interventions with kids about to go away for life. Gary and Colleen's support went way beyond the clinical realm. They had adopted twenty-eight of the young men.

"How do you do it?" I asked. "How do you work with them?"

I sensed that Gary and Colleen's efficacy with the court-referred boys had a lot to do with their sparkling, radiating love and, as they'd intimated after the talk, with spiritual awareness. The rest of the table was engaged in an academic discussion on research paradigms and statistical models and where to publish their next articles, but all I wanted to talk about was how Gary and Colleen Weaver helped people.

"We go out in the desert," Gary said vaguely, eyes twinkling. "I'll show you sometime."

Dessert was served, and then guests began to leave, tossing their white linen napkins on chairs and tabletops. Gary, Colleen, and I were the last ones seated, lingering even after the dessert plates were cleared.

"Can you show me now?" I asked quietly. "How do you teach spiritual awareness?"

"It's not through a particular religion," Gary said. "Most of these boys we work with have had bad scrapes with the messengers of religion."

He was quiet a moment, then snapped his fingers. "Let's do it!"

He led me in this transcendent visualization exercise, called Holding Council:

Sit down. Close your eyes.

Set before you a table. To your table you may invite anyone, living or deceased, who truly has your best interest in mind.

With all of your guests sitting there at your table, ask them if they love you.

And now to your table, invite your higher self. The part of you that is much greater than anything you've done or not done, anything you have or don't have.

Ask your eternal, higher self if you love you.

And now to your table invite your higher power, whoever or whatever it is to you. Ask if your higher power loves you.

And now, with all of those people sitting there, right now, ask, "What do I need to know right now? What do they need to tell me?"

It was a fast track to *awakened connection*. To realizing that we are in relationships—with our ancestors, our loved ones, our higher selves, our higher power—that transcend physical presence, and through which we gain something vital and useful. Your inner council is always there. Different people may show up at your table at different times. You can ask them questions anytime, anywhere.

I've done this exercise now countless times, with students, parents, business leaders, lawyers, people in tech and finance, and without fail they seem enlivened and comforted by it. In elite institutions and professions, people are accustomed to thinking in terms of competition and comparison, and often their lives have been made brittle through this unrelenting self-assessment. In just a few quiet, contemplative minutes they wake up to how much they're loved, how much others, including those long-forgotten or departed, are with them.

As I kept discovering in my clinical work, engaging this awareness of loving connection enables profound healing. I witnessed it again when I was asked to design a clinical intervention at Covenant House, a shelter for at-risk homeless youth on the West Side of Manhattan, near the Lincoln Tunnel. The shelter provides temporary living accommodations and assistance with career development to youth transitioning out of foster care or unstable home environments.

"My world is a house where every door I open is filled with more fire," Randy, a twenty-year-old man, said at the beginning of the group therapy course. His life had been constantly ruptured by disconnection. He had been born in Trinidad, abandoned by his father when he was very young, and now had fraught relationships with his mother and sister, with whom he had moved to New York. He no longer lived with them, and they rarely spoke. He experienced severe anxiety, was on the borderline for a diagnosis of major depressive disorder, and was highly reactive. He was unable to listen to any criticism, and had extreme conflict in his relationships. When our team first saw Randy, he was on the phone, screaming at his girlfriend at the top of his lungs. Anger was how he vented his pain and tried to control his environment. He also self-medicated with frequent drug use.

Randy stated three goals for the group therapy, which would consist of a weekly two-hour group session supplemented by open-door individual therapy sessions: *I plan to learn more ways to overcome my distress and anger and transform it into something or anything worth something,* he wrote. *I have a new job starting tomorrow and my main goal is to maintain this job by working hard every day.* He also stated that he wanted to learn to *build better relationships. I feel that it will help me as a person to learn to love people for who they are and not necessarily what they do.*

Each group session began with a relaxation exercise and a guided visualization. Physiologically speaking, these practices would calm the nervous system, quiet achieving awareness, and ready participants to come at their healing with more ease and less reactivity. When all the participants had gathered in the conference room at Covenant House, they each found a space on the floor to sit peacefully and close their eyes. Lorne, my doctoral student, who had worked with Gary and Colleen Weaver's youth in the desert, would turn off the fluorescent lights and use a Tibetan Buddhist sound bowl, similar to those many mystical traditions use to facilitate relaxation and meditation, to set the tone for practice.

As the vibrations filled the space, our team asked the young men to focus on breathing deeply in and out, filling the abdomen and then the chest, releasing completely. Inherently calming, the process also brought about a state of entrainment through the use of sound, similar to the brain-wave entrainment in Jacobo Grinberg's and Andy Newberg's studies. The vibration pattern of the singing bowl caused the participants' brain waves to synchronize with the sound waves in a deeply relaxing pattern—the equivalent of REM cycle number 1, theta.

The next part of the exercise took them even further into a spiritual experience. The young men were guided to visualize opening their hearts, and to feel love flowing naturally into their hearts, mounting and mounting till they felt that they were full of love; then they sent love through their hearts to a fellow young man in the circle. This experience of sending and receiving love built a felt awakened connection. Then, from a place of feeling love, with their eyes still closed, they were asked to create a mental picture of their higher self, the part of us that's beyond what we have or don't have, what we achieve or don't achieve. It's our pure essence, our core being, untarnished by our mistakes or deprivations, by what we do to others or what's been done to us. We asked them to imagine their current self receiving loving-kindness from their higher self. This active intention of love toward self was challenging for many. Negative core beliefs—of damage, isolation, or worthlessness—emerged in the process of trying to offer themselves love. But over time, they became better at receiving and reciprocating love, growing to see themselves as inherently good and worthy of love, and became more aware of their connection and resonance with others.

As the young men experienced unmediated resonance with their higher selves and with one another, changes were visible, even early in the program. After a few weeks, Randy appeared less angry and walled-off. He said he felt like he had more "water" at his disposal—he was literally spending more time near the water, walking along the Hudson after work—and he had more tools to quell the fire of his anger. By the ninth week, he told us he wanted to try to repair his relationship with his girlfriend. He said he planned to ask her for forgiveness, and communicate his feelings of love and care for her.

When he came to the next group session, he was euphoric, his spine tall, his eyes full of light. She had forgiven him. Their relationship was back on solid footing. It was the first time he'd experienced a positive resolution to a conflict, and the first time he'd managed a conflict through expressions of love and emotional vulnerability rather than anger.

But the next week, his anger took over again. Other residents at the shelter who were not in the group therapy program instigated a fight and goaded Randy into participating. He was on the verge of pummeling one of the other residents when a fellow group therapy member managed to talk him down and stop the fight. At the next session, we talked about the conflict—why it had erupted, and how the usual violence had been avoided. The young men talked about how easy it was for the stresses and demands of their environment to unravel their progress. They said they often felt like crabs in a bucket, each preventing the others from trying to escape. They also said they were learning how important it was to transcend the pressure to conform to the culture of anger and violence; to open their hearts, send and receive love, and build and sustain awakened connection.

One young man put it powerfully. "That guy," he said, pointing to a young man sitting across the room on the floor. "We used to hate each other. We were in opposite gangs. But now, he's my brother, and we love each other. When we did that visualization today, I sent him love." He hit his chest. The other man hit his chest in return. It was incredibly powerful to witness these strong and hardened young men exchanging deep feelings of forgiveness, respect, and love.

By the end of the program, there were significant decreases in participants' symptoms of distress and levels of depression and general anxiety, and clear improvements in their overall interpersonal functioning. The participants had come to the therapy program suffering in a world of separateness, feeling angry and oppositional toward other people and the world at large. And they had gone through a process that awakened them to a different way of being, to a feeling of oneness and connection even with rival gang members or people from whom they'd been estranged.

The last time we saw Randy, he had been promoted to manager of the copy shop where he'd started working at the start of the group therapy course. His scores on the clinical scales had fallen from clinically significant levels to nonclinical levels, and he said his feelings of anger "went from the ceiling to the floor."

"There's more," he said. "Guess who I called on Sunday? My mom. I hadn't talked to her in a long time, but I called to wish her a happy Mother's Day."

OVER AND OVER—from the *inipi* in South Dakota to a judge's chambers in Russia, from entrainment studies to Gary and Colleen Weaver's twenty-eight sons—I was encountering the same finding: awakened relationships transform and heal. Instead of feeling in opposition to others, or in competition, isolation, or anger, we have infinitely more options for how we relate. Life and lab were revealing the same thing: that we're bonded in a network of love, that life itself holds us in a loving embrace.

And . . . I was also profoundly, unfathomably tired. Phil and I both were. In ten months, Leah hadn't slept through a single night. Our opportunities for rest were chopped and scattered like confetti. Isaiah was a little over two, a wild and darting toddler. Leah was already starting to pull herself up, and it was only a matter of time before she and Isaiah would both be running fast. My brain hurt from exhaustion, and also from the tight grip of attention required to keep both little ones in my line of sight, to prevent them from choking on a marble or falling into a ditch. Phil was so exhausted that he'd leave the house and drive, just to drive, to have that open, expansive attention with no noises or needs or intrusions.

He was out driving one afternoon, the kids building and toppling block towers on the rug, when my mother called from Boston.

"I had a dream," she said. "There were three car seats in the back seat of your car."

I laughed. A third child? It had taken five years to conceive Leah. And how would we manage? It seemed the only rest I got was in line at the coffee shop. Every other waking moment, if I wasn't working, my head was an unceasing narration to keep myself on track: *Lift your hand, turn on the water, fill the pot, put it on the stove, shake noodles out of the box.* It already took everything I had to keep from driving into the median on my way home.

And yet, while fatigue narrowed my lens, my children were direct portals to awakened awareness. They brought me to the most soaring and euphoric love—not only *for* them, but *with* them, *through* them. They connected me to something bigger.

To all of life. I held Isaiah and Leah in utter awe—and it wasn't just their profound and beautiful beings that rushed me with warmth. It was the quality of their presence and awareness. Like the indigenous healers in Achterberg's study, my babies were the ultimate in resonance and entrainment. Their perceptual capacities awakened mine. Like the day we'd brought Isaiah home and sat him by the river and he'd reached for us to share his wonder. Or the times I'd lie in bed with Leah by my side and she would look at me with a love so blinding I felt almost unworthy to return her gaze. And yet, loving my children had taught me that we're all worthy of love—that love is our birthright. It's how we're built to send and receive. The exhaustion was real. And so was the vast guidance and love, the connection between and beyond us. The exhaustion wasn't a wall that blocked my path—it was an opening to something much bigger and more profound than I'd ever known.

When I woke suddenly that night, reflexively listening for Leah's cry, the house was quiet. I heard Phil's breathing, the rush of the river outside. Then the dark room seemed to open up. I could sense the sacred profundity coming. First a numinous, glowing quality, then that deep, intense presence that had visited me two times before.

Do you want me to come? it said.

As before, my response was immediate, intuitive, as free and natural as an exhale.

"Yes, very much," I said.

Does Phil want me to come? it said.

If I'd answered with my head, if I'd made a list of pros and cons, measuring the space in our hearts against the circles under his eyes, I might have paused. But I answered with my heart. "Very much," I said.

The glow dissipated. My heart calmed. I was nearly back to

sleep when Phil woke and turned to me. We were so tired during those months, it was rare for us to reach for each other. But that night he woke and came to me.

In the morning, trying to keep Isaiah out of the dog's water bowl, wiping spilled milk and Cheerios off the high chair, I felt it deep in my being. Our third child was on her way.

CHAPTER 16

AWAKENED HEART

From the day she was born, our third child, Lila, was unflappable. Her mighty, realist nature was visible from the start. We were in the hospital, recovering after her birth, and Phil came in to check on us, clearly overwhelmed by the scene at home and the prospect of bringing a newborn into the mix.

"Well, you look rested," he grumbled. He paced the hospital room, then said, "I'm getting a coffee," and left in a huff.

"Oh, Lila," I said, gazing at her rosy little face, "what are we going to do?"

She looked right back with unflinching readiness, as if to say, "Hey, we're great!"

She didn't get riled. She would become the only person in the family who could shake Phil out of a funk—she'd parody his dour, ruminative, self-critical moods by shuffling around with her lips pursed, sternly shaking her head, saying, "No, no, not good at all," until he burst out laughing. Lila was born ready to see the light and dark, the good and bad, and then choose the bright side. She was fearless, with a joyful, game-for-it smile that could bring anyone on board.

WHEN GARY WEAVER died in March 2014, it was Lila who traveled with me to the funeral, where we gathered in his church in a tiny town in the hot Utah desert. Hundreds of people came to his funeral; the back of the church had to be opened up to create more space—and still there wasn't enough room. Lila was beside me, in a frilly dress over what she called "action shorts," kneeling backward on the seat, belly pressed against the back of the pew.

"Mama," she said, surveying the room. "There's a lot of people here."

"Yes," I said. "Gary touched many people's lives." I asked her if she remembered when Gary and Colleen had visited us in Connecticut. They'd listened attentively to Lila as she gave an extensive recitation of details about her nursery school classmates, Gary later pulling out a harmonica and playing for us while we danced.

The last time I'd brought her to the Utah desert she'd shot off fearlessly to climb the structures at Arches National Park, hanging upside down on forty-foot-tall inverted forms, so at home and free in the open landscape that I had to hang a whistle around her neck so I could locate her in the vast desert. She was an adventurer at heart—forging the river at high season, running alone and barefoot through the rocky high hills near our house, thrilling to find "secret forts" where a fox might be living—but I'd attributed some of her ease in the desert to her time spent with Gary and Colleen, sharing in their way of being. Gary had always said that God is in the desert.

Now the first two rows were filling with the twenty-eight

young men Gary and Colleen had adopted, the court-referred boys they had raised and helped guide. They were now in their thirties and forties: husbands and fathers, teachers, environmentalists, therapists, and businesspeople. If not for Gary Weaver's intervention, they might still be languishing in prison, isolated from the relationships and contributions that had become so important and sustaining for themselves and their communities. My former graduate student Lorne sat among them.

Back when Lorne was still a doctoral student, our initial collaborative EEG study at Columbia had revealed that people who recover from depression through a deepened spirituality give off a posterior high-amplitude alpha wavelength—the same wavelength given off posteriorly in some practices by meditating monks. I was curious where else in nature this wavelength was found and asked Lorne to help me find out. I had asked him, "What is it in nature, a tree, a leaf, an animal, that vibrates at alpha?" Lorne showed up at my office a week later with a bright smile. "Alpha is everywhere," he said. He showed me research beginning as early as 1893 that examined what are now called Schumann resonances, a set of spectrum peaks in the extremely low frequencies in the Earth's electromagnetic field spectrum. Alpha is a resonance in the space between the Earth's crust to one mile up, set and reset by lightning and other activity in the ionosphere. High-amplitude alpha is everywhere. The same wavelength of brains in meditation or prayer, and shared by the men and women holding hands in times of pain, is the wavelength of the oneness of all life. The brain-to-brain coupling site by which we perceive ourselves on common ground with fellow humans is also that through which we perceive oneness with God, nature, or the universe. All these forms of unitive awareness, of moving from a point to a wave—whether shared with people, nature, or a higher power—involve energy at alpha frequency. **When we awaken, we resonate at the same frequency as all of nature on Earth.** We rejoin life.

Gary Weaver taught that the universe is conscious and loving, and he'd modeled a way to live in alignment with that resonance, to transform through love and belonging, to reconstrue who we are to one another.

At the end of the service, twenty-eight pallbearers rose to carry the coffin. We gathered outside, the brown, yellow, orange, and pink of the mountains around us. One of Gary's pallbearers and sons told me how he had found Gary: "When I was growing up, I couldn't be in my house. It was abusive. Angry. I would ride my bike all day, just to be away. There was this house that I would stop outside because I could always hear people laughing and there was always music. It was Gary's house. He played the harmonica, and I would just stand outside with my bike, sometimes for an hour. I never dreamt that years later Gary would adopt me."

Gary had shown me and countless others that we have an inner instrument, and it has many channels; we can use our own volitional inner practice like an antenna to access the conscious and loving world around us. When we do, we're less depressed, addicted, and anxious, and more connected. An awakened heart is the seat of our unity with all life.

LIVING ONLY IN achieving awareness, relationships tend to be transactional. We look at people in terms of how they've helped or harmed us. And our decisions tend to be unilateral, motivated by self-interest. An awakened heart gives us another possibility—to make decisions and seek solutions that serve the individual and the common good.

Bob Chapman, chairman and CEO of Barry-Wehmiller, a

St. Louis–based global supplier of manufacturing technology and services, shows how his business leadership evolved—and his success accelerated—when he approached leadership with an awakened heart.

Chapman has what he describes as a very traditional business education—BS in accounting from Indiana University, MBA from the University of Michigan, and two years at Price Waterhouse before joining Barry-Wehmiller in 1969—and he spent the first half of his career doing what he learned to do in business school: use others for his personal success.

"I needed an engineer, or a receptionist, and I paid them to do a job. I might have been nice to them," Chapman said, "but when I did not need them anymore, I let them go in order to cut cost and improve profits, as that was our singular measure."

His transformation was significantly influenced by a wedding in Aspen, Colorado, as he watched his friend walk his precious daughter down the aisle.

"That's when it hit me," Chapman said. "The twelve thousand people who work for Barry-Wehmiller around the world, whom I had been seeing as functions for the business's success, as engineers, accountants, assemblers, machine operators, expediters—I was awakened to the realization that each of them is someone's precious child, just like the young lady and young man who were getting married that day. My role as a leader was to help Barry-Wehmiller employees discover, develop, share, and be appreciated for their gifts while they were in my care."

Yet the vast majority of people in this country—88 percent—feel they work in an organization that does not care about them. Chapman said, "We came to realize that the way our team members are treated at work has a profound impact on the way they return home and treat their spouses and children."

His awakening can be summed up by one simple statement:

"I want to send people home fulfilled, knowing that who they are and what they do matters."

He sees his role much differently now; instead of managing people for his own success, he strives to create human value in harmony with economic value, driven by this leadership vision: "We measure success by the way we touch the lives of people."

When his dad died and Chapman took over the company, it was near bankruptcy. Banks pulled out on them, and he faced a dramatic challenge. He went to the VP of finance with a plan: to look for acquisitions and new products so they could build a better future in better markets. The VP of finance said, "Yeah, great idea, Bob. But there's a problem. We have no money." Unencumbered by the lack of funds or experience, Chapman committed to finding opportunities that would diversify the struggling business.

"What do you buy when you have no money?" he said. "The businesses nobody else wants. The ones they're basically giving away."

He bought a number of companies that appeared broke on paper. Two years later, he carried out a massively successful IPO on the London Stock Exchange that was thirty-five times oversubscribed, and in the early nineties, Harvard Business School wrote a case study on this dramatic transformation.

It has often been times of great challenge that have brought opportunities for growth. During the 2008 financial crisis, when new orders were scarce, a $30 million order on the backlog was suddenly put on hold, and Chapman was faced with deploying the traditional practice of downsizing to make up for the significant drop in revenue.

"No CEO likes downsizing and letting people go, but it goes with the job to strive to meet the profit expectation of investors," Chapman says. "However, we knew that entire towns would suffer if we downsized significantly, so we asked, 'What would a caring family do if a family member was in crisis?' They would pitch together and all take a little pain so that no one person took all the pain." Chapman reduced his annual salary to ten thousand dollars—his starting salary out of college. And he asked everyone in the company to take one month of unpaid vacation. Instead of cutting costs by laying people off, everyone kept their jobs, further validating the caring culture he was striving to create.

Something completely unexpected happened. Because employees felt secure and cared for, they started spontaneously caring for one another, some people taking an extra week or two of unpaid leave so that someone else could keep working.

"We didn't tell people to be altruistic," Chapman says. "But caring is contagious." People were willing to give up that month's salary to help a fellow team member. The company survived the extraordinary economic challenge—and, as important, the way Bob and the team responded validated that they cared.

A company culture rooted in care need not be at odds with profit. Under Chapman's leadership, Barry-Wehmiller has grown from an $18 million company into a $3 billion global company with more than 115 acquisitions. In 2017, Chapman was named the country's #3 CEO by *Inc.,* and the company's compound growth in share value has increased well over 10 percent a year since 1997.

But the external measures of success pale in comparison to an inner sense of connection and inherent worth. At a time when the company was growing dramatically and Barry-Wehmiller's success story was being touted in the national business community, Chapman remembers telling his pastor, "You know, I'm not sure I believe in God." Without hesitation, his pastor looked at him and said, "Bob, the good news is, he believes in you."

Bob replied with a smile: "I thought I was here to validate

God." Instead, he was struck by an understanding of unconditional love and the awesome responsibility he feels to those he has the privilege to lead.

The unconditional love to which Chapman was awakened is a significant component of spirituality among diverse global traditions and cultures. In 2016, I received a generous private grant to research universal dimensions of spirituality, and my team (with elegant translation and data acquisition design by doctoral students Clayton McClintock and Elsa Lau) started by studying 5,500 participants in India, China, and the United States. Among our participants, who represented the most populous world religious traditions—Christianity, Islam, Hinduism, Buddhism—as well as the category of nonreligious, secular, or spiritual-but-not-religious, we found that people shared five common spiritual phenotypes:

1. Altruism
2. Love of Neighbor as Self
3. Sense of Oneness
4. Practice of Sacred Transcendence
5. Adherence to Moral Code

Across humanity we find magnificently vivid and diverse expressions of spiritual life, told in varied languages, stories, and symbols, and experienced in ceremony, ritual, transcendent practice, and other sacred ways of coming together. This rich diversity in spirituality stems from the two-thirds of our spiritual contribution that is passed through the teachings of generations and learned through the environment. Our study took into account the diverse expressions of spirituality, and gave us a clearer picture of the one-third heritable contribution to our shared spiritual capacity. The five universal phenotypes clarified that while the formation of spirituality is impacted by diverse cultures and traditions, the seat of spiritual perception is innate. Ultimately, we can share and feel spiritual experiences at a deep level, with the "knowing of the heart," right across the so-called lines of faith traditions, because we are all built with the same foundationally spiritual brain.

Our research had already shown that spirituality is deep in our nature, in our brains, inside us. Now we had a more descriptive way of defining what it means to be spiritual. The Unit 6 patients at the makeshift Yom Kippur service, the New Haven youth experiencing moments of transcendence in nature or prayer, the young men at Covenant House connecting with their higher selves, Iliana in the wake of her father's death, Kathleen as she reoriented after divorce—each person was tapping into aspects of spiritual awareness that are universal and innate.

Once we'd identified the five universal spiritual phenotypes, I wondered if we could get more specific about spirituality in the brain. Could each phenotype be mapped to a particular neurocorrelate? Given the overall structural benefits of the awakened brain, could we determine which of the five spiritual phenotypes were most protective against cortical thinning and depression?

We returned to collaborate with Myrna Weissman on her beautiful longitudinal data set, this time looking at more than seventy adults aged twenty-two to sixty-three, the second- and third-generation offspring of the depressed and non-depressed women in her original cohort. For each participant, her team had again taken MRI scans of both left and right hemispheres of the brain at year thirty of the study, which meant we could look at how the brain structure was related to personal spirituality and symptoms of depression over time. Using survey questions mapped to the spiritual phenotypes, we gave each participant a "spiritual phenotype factor score" for each of the five phenotypes, and examined the association between cortical thickness in spiritual regions of the brain, symptoms and diagnoses of depression, and phenotype factor scores.

We made an important discovery. There was enhanced cortical thickness—in other words, structural protection against depression—in the participants who were both high-risk for depression and had a relatively stronger sense of the first two phenotypes, altruism and love of neighbor as self (with the phenotype of oneness present, but with a variable statistical signal). The same neural protective benefits were *not* seen in people at low risk for depression or associated with the other spiritual phenotypes.

More specifically, altruism and love of neighbor correlated with cortical thickness across the spiritual network of the brain, including regions of bonding, suggesting a robust protective benefit of **relational spirituality**, a personal spirituality that emphasizes both our commitment to other humans and our awareness of a transcendent or higher power—and how *divine and human love are linked*. Our finding touched on the cornerstone of all faith traditions: that sacred, transcendent love ignites in service to one another. What we saw in the scanner suggested a neuroanatomical foundation to relational spirituality. Here may be the bedrock of human possibility, where the secular humanists and evangelicals meet in ultimate significance and service to the world.

We saw that the people at high risk for depression who were also high in altruism and love of neighbor had a decreased relative risk for depression. This finding implies that relational spirituality interventions focusing on altruism and love could benefit people at high risk for depression, offering a pathway to resil ience. What's more, we found that for people at high risk for depression, altruism and love of neighbor are *prospectively* protective against depressive symptoms. In other words, people high in altruism and love are less depressed years in the future than those who are less altruistic, with an even bigger effect if they have been depressed in the past. If you take Prozac to treat depression, and then stop taking the medication, you could potentially be depressed again within a matter of weeks. But our study suggested that daily, lived altruism may be curative.

Why does altruism—lived, actionable service to fellow humans—prevent against the downward spiral of recurrent depression among people with a lifelong tendency to suffer? Maybe because it draws people out of isolation and into reconnection, benefiting both the helper and the helped. Maybe because it fulfills a sense of purpose and gives expression to deep calling and contribution. Maybe because it restores us to ourselves—to our own optimum functioning, and also to an accurate perception of the nature of life. We rise from the narrows of splintered self-interest, isolation, and competition, and awaken our hearts to the world as it is.

And the world flourishes with us. Our own optimum functioning is good for others and the earth. The very same way of being that creates a healthy, interconnected brain generates the most interconnected state of humanity and all life. The awakened brain enables us to see our connection to others and to Earth—and it guides us, even requires us, to live in a way that supports that connection. Altruism is essentially an embodied form of our awareness of unity and love. Our awareness and our way of being become integrated and mutually enforcing, altruism both the conduit and destination of our awakening, a lived expression of who we are to one another.

This is perhaps the biggest revelation of the awakened brain: that **it's in our innate nature to build a better world**. That what's good for everyone is also what's best for each one of us.

WHEN WE ACTIVATE altruism, we engage neural functioning essential to our personal wellness and thriving—and to the wellness and thriving of all. Everyone gains when we open our hearts to others and to all life.

Tim Shriver, chairman of Special Olympics and a member of the prominent American Kennedy family, shares how an awakened heart helped him transform a sense of fragmentation into a perception of unity, and how the spiritual perception of oneness influences his work and activism now.

The sense of dichotomy and fragmentation began early in his life, when his experience of play, harmony, and togetherness was pierced by "shocking, lifelong, unprocessable grief and loss" following the assassinations of his uncles, John and Robert Kennedy. He didn't know how to hold the losses alongside the peace.

This sense of fracture continued as he began a career in urban education. Many of the kids he worked with were deeply wounded, pained, and grieving.

"I was mesmerized," he said, "because I felt like we had so much in common. It looked like I was a rich white kid with a college education and money and privilege and all the things that on the surface, of course, I am. But emotionally, I was with those kids strolling the streets at night, not wanting to go to school, not knowing how to make sense of the world or understand why anything at all mattered."

But he didn't know how to help them—or himself—heal the sense of irrelevance. "I just kept telling them not to listen to their own inner voices," Shriver says. "I'd tell them, 'Do your home-work, work harder, try harder, get your grades up. I can help you get a two-car garage and a house in the suburbs. And, dammit, do your homework.' And they kept telling me, 'No, that's a lie. That doesn't produce the outcome I'm looking for. Not even close.' And they were right. It was a lie for them. It is for all of us."

When he was twenty-five, heartbroken over a lost love, in New Haven and looking for a place to live after the roommates he'd had the year before finished law school and architecture school and moved to New York and Boston, the pastor at Saint Martin de Porres invited him to rent a room at the rectory.

He attended parish functions, helping to serve food and clean up. One evening a parishioner introduced him to a book on centering prayer and the idea that there's oneness within each of us.

"To reveal, touch, and become receptive to a oneness that already exists?" Shriver said. "It was completely foreign to me."

But he was curious. One night he sat in the chapel alone with all but the altar lights out, his eyes closed, trying to be present and silent in the space. After what felt like an eternity, but was probably only three or four minutes, he opened his eyes and be-came immediately transfixed by the floor-to-ceiling mural be-hind the altar of Saint Martin, a mendicant monk of color who was treated badly in the monastery. In the mural, he's outside, feeding the poor with scraps from the monastery. Shriver was flooded by impressions.

"First, this saint was just a guy. All he ever did was be himself; he did nothing grand or big, accomplished nothing in the ways I had always thought I was supposed to. It was both enormously sad—I felt so sorry for the humiliation and rejection he'd experienced—and enormously freeing. He's a saint hundreds of years after his death. For what reason? For nothing he earned. He didn't have to do anything extraordinary. He just had to let his heart be open and do the work of love and justice that was given to him to do, however simple. If he had crumbs and scraps to give, he gave crumbs and scraps. And that was enough."

In that moment, he felt a freedom he hadn't known existed, a freedom he never knew was there to seek. It was a feeling of oneness, a sense of being safe in his own presence in that little church, and the feeling that a new path had opened up for him. There was a new road to travel. A new way to be a teacher, an advocate, a person of wholeness. The goal of earning approval and success for himself or his students yielded to a new goal: to be present to the gift of each of his students and to focus on unleashing each child's sense of their own goodness and light.

In the years that followed, Shriver became convinced that his shift in heart and focus was a shift that could help all educators and children too. He joined with colleagues and helped found the social and emotional learning movement in education—an effort to train teachers and children to be self-aware, learn empathy, practice positive decision making, and develop a sense of agency and power based on the universal dignity of every person. Later, his journey led him to serve as chairman of the board for Special Olympics, and to work on transcending what he calls "othering"—the shaming, guilt, scapegoating, and stigmatizing most of us unconsciously practice in an effort to feel safety and belonging.

He says the most consistent dimension of his spiritual awareness is the recognition of how often he still gets it wrong—how often he misses the warm, full embrace of oneness. On a recent trip to Germany, he met with Chancellor Angela Merkel and spoke at the Bundestag. After a day of hearings and press releases, he went out to dinner with a dozen colleagues. They gathered around one table in a noisy restaurant. A German Special Olympics athlete was sitting across from Shriver, and a professor was next to him.

"He was a St. Thomas scholar," Shriver says, "and I was excitedly talking to him about Aristotle and Thomas, having this scholarly, academic conversation."

The athlete, Philippe, was silent through the meal. A few times Shriver tried to draw him into the conversation, but Philippe just smiled.

At the end of the meal, Shriver rose to make a toast. As he thanked everyone for coming, he noticed Philippe sitting quietly, and asked if he wanted to say anything.

"He just looked at me. I wasn't sure how much English he understood, so I invited him again to say a few words, speaking slowly, enunciating as clearly as I could. He looked around the room. He smiled at everybody. And then he said, in fragmented English, 'I want to say big, big, big thank you, everyone. Big, big.' And I burst into tears. I was so embarrassed. Words weren't the important thing. I'd spent an hour talking about some bullshit academic theory relevant only to my desire to feel more important or valuable or worthy because I have the capacity to talk about bullshit theories. And here was Philippe, embodying everything that's actually important: being gentle, and present, and vulnerable, and overwhelmingly loving to everybody. I'd just missed the damn point."

Shriver says his work constantly invites him to discern whether or not he's a hypocrite.

"Do I actually believe that this person with intellectual disabilities who is sitting at the table with me is a beautiful child of

God, equal to every other form of life that's ever existed? Or am I subtly falling prey to the trap that rich people or smart people or pretty people or skilled people are better?"

This is the challenge that belongs to each of us: We can see people as other. Or we can see the all.

Shriver says that America is suffering from a spiritual crisis; we've collapsed into corrosive and epidemic levels of othering. He calls for radical social change that emanates from a deep, felt experience of love and belonging, an awakened awareness of who we are to one another, a hunger for justice rooted in the transformative power of wholeness and dignity.

"Spiritual ways of knowing have been crushed by binary ways of knowing," he said. "Toxic judgment is so prevalent we almost don't notice it."

We think in terms of binaries and divisions. Red state/Blue state. Nationalist/Immigrant. White/Black. Queer/Straight. Even efforts to acknowledge and celebrate our individuality and differences can become narrow and splintered.

"We end up in bubbles with very narrow bands of language and experience that too often slip into individualistic self-interest," Shriver says. "You talk to people who know and like you and think like you, and you don't talk to other people. It's a pursuit of safety and belonging that is more likely to be a recipe for loneliness and fear that is too often directed against some other. And sadly, the narrower the bubbles we live in, the more that fear and hatred of others grow, making the work of justice and peace almost impossible."

Needless to say, nothing is impossible for the spirit! Healing comes when we end othering—when we find a language and a way to be with one another that allows us to transcend division and embrace our shared hunger for meaning, value, connection, and hope. That's the means to achieve the justice and respect that are so absent today—a practiced willingness to cross boundaries of division, refuse contempt, and acknowledge the dignity of others. Then, justice has a chance.

This means we acknowledge grief—and there is so much unresolved grief in our culture. Shriver said, "We have to be able to find solidarity with one another when our hearts break, and sadness overwhelms us, and we feel darkness on the horizon and the looming loneliness that comes from losing what we love, what we no longer can have, which is forever taken from us. We must find the way to speak our truth and release the pain, and in that release, discover the source, the strength, the hope that sustains us. We must look into the depths of our own souls, face that pain with all of its horror and difficulty, and know somehow, somewhere, in some deep sense, we will be okay."

And this means we have to learn to talk in a new way. That our collective discourse must become full of spiritual questions: *What inspires you to believe in something bigger than yourself? What's the greatest hope you have lingering and surging from your heart? What participation do you see for yourself in the future yet to be imagined?*

And we must remember that as long as there is a single person on the margin, we are not one.

Shriver said, "The secret opportunity in front of us is the chance to not only help but to heal. To not be crushed by discomfort. To navigate a path where we can both listen deeply to the wisdom of the margins and seek justice together without creating new divisions."

AN AWAKENED HEART can lead us to a world with less social division and marginalization—and it can heal our relationship with the planet.

When Leah and Isaiah were young and I was newly pregnant

with Lila, Phil and I hired a babysitter one afternoon and headed out for a lunch at the local diner. It was February, cold and austere, the trees bare, dirty snow plowed into hills on the sides of the road. About a mile away from home, at a tricky intersection, I saw three young deer in their first winter, clustered tightly together, starkly staring, no mother to be seen. I felt an immediate connection with and concern for the deer, three lost children. Worried that they didn't know what to eat, or that there was simply not enough food on the branches, I sent them a message from my heart, mentally telling them, *I will feed you.* My achieving brain quickly retaliated, chastising, *How will they ever find you?* But the next day, there they were, all three arriving in my driveway at the exact moment I walked outdoors into the cold. They stared right at me. We had connected in the field of the awakened heart. I strongly suspect that the connection could have been picked up as alpha in an EEG, either on them or on me.

Ilias Kamitsis, a professor of ecotherapy at the University of Melbourne, while examining the ways in which exposure and connectedness to nature are positively associated with both psychological well-being and greater reported spirituality, discovered that spiritual awareness actually *mediates* the relationship between psychological well-being and our experience in nature. The awakened brain amplifies the way we relate to nature—and it heightens the benefits we derive from that connection.

Mary Evelyn Tucker, professor of world religions and ecology at Yale, says that we're at a breakthrough moment in human development. Science reveals that we are living, evolving creatures within the context of a living, evolving planet and universe. For example, the new field of biosemiotics investigates how forests think and communicate. Whether we're looking at river or forest systems, individual cells, or the birth of the cosmos, we see a portrait of the world and all living things that is fundamentally relational, reciprocal, and interconnected. Indigenous peoples have understood this interdependence for millennia. Now an awareness of our place in the universe gives us the imperative to restore our rivers, forests, wetlands, shorelines, and degraded spaces, and transcend rampant materialism and exploitation of our resources. It also gives us the hope, awe, wonder, and beauty we need for the work ahead—a sense of our belonging to something much larger than ourselves, of our place within and contribution to a huge, evolving, unfolding fourteen-billion-year-old story.

STEVEN CLARK ROCKEFELLER, a fourth-generation Rocke-feller and the oldest living male member of the family, is a prime example of how an awakened heart and ethical leadership can merge in concrete actions that better the world. His grandfather, John D. Rockefeller, Jr., who had a strong influence on Steven, was guided by a liberal Christian faith and committed to a life of philanthropy in an effort to expunge from the family name the image of the "robber baron" placed on his father, the founder of the Standard Oil Company. Fundamental to his grandfather's understanding of how a family should manage great wealth was a demanding ethical guideline clearly articulated in his credo: "I believe that every right implies a responsibility; every opportunity, an obligation; every possession, a duty."

Conservation was a major philanthropic interest of John D. Jr., and he played a leading role in the creation of five national parks, including Acadia National Park in Maine and Grand Teton National Park in Wyoming, where Steven spent summers during his childhood.

"My experiences in nature touched me very deeply," he says, "and awakened a sense that there is a sacred presence in and through all things."

The Teton Range had an especially powerful impact. Steven's first visit to the area was in 1946, when he was twelve. Two years later he took his first paying job, working for the foreman on his grandfather's ranch in the Tetons. When he was sixteen, he worked as the wrangler on the ranch. When he was eighteen, he got a summer job with the National Park Service working on a four-man trail crew, living in a tent deep in the mountains at elevations between 9,000 and 10,000 feet.

"It was a joy to be alive and working surrounded by the magical beauty of those majestic mountains with their snow fields, glacier lakes, wildflower meadows, rushing streams, deep forests, and moose, bear, and other wildlife," remarks Steven. Such experiences have remained with him over the years as vivid memories, and inspired by the commitment of his grandfather and his uncle Laurance Rockefeller to preserving places of great natural beauty and their biological diversity, he became actively engaged in the environmental movement.

The immersion of his father, Nelson Rockefeller, in international affairs and their extensive travels together became another touchpoint of awakened awareness. He remembers in particular a two-month-long journey they took through fourteen countries in Africa. He had just finished his junior year in college, and it was at a time when his father was beginning to think seriously about running for president. They started the trip in Liberia on the west coast, traveled down to South Africa, and ended up in Kenya and Egypt. "It was 1957 and the colonial era was coming to an end. All over Africa, people were aspiring to independence, and many were actively preparing for it. South Africa was still in the grip of apartheid, and the social tension and fear were palpable," recalls Steven. "When we arrived in Cairo, the British were poised to seize control of the Suez Canal and armed soldiers were on alert throughout the city."

Traveling with his family in Africa, Asia, Europe, and Latin America made him keenly aware of the international community and its great cultural diversity and of how each of us is part of the larger human family. "These trips were the beginning of my growing consciousness of the world—the planet—as a living, interdependent whole," he says.

During the 1960s Steven pursued graduate studies at Union Theological Seminary and Columbia University, deepening his understanding of Christian theology and ethics and the history of philosophy and the world's religions. Fascinated by the writings of the mystics and seeking to explore more fully the spiritual dimension of experience, as he began his teaching career in the 1970s he also plunged into Zen Buddhist training in meditation. He was particularly moved and inspired by the first of the four vows taken by Zen practitioners: "All beings without number I vow to liberate."

"This vow," explains Steven, "is an expression of interconnection and compassionate identification with all life, which is the heart of the Bodhisattva spiritual ideal in Zen Buddhism. Zen practice is not about seeking one's own salvation or liberation as an individual separate from everyone else. It is about waking up to the deeper truth that we are one human family and one Earth community with a common destiny, and that meaning and fulfillment are found in and through keeping our hearts open, nurturing caring relationships, and contributing according to our ability to the well-being of the larger whole of which we are all interdependent members. Zen teaches that one should strive for enlightenment, not for oneself, but so that one can better help others and avoid harming them."

What attracted Steven to Zen is in part what he had experienced as a boy in nature: a deep sense of interconnection with the larger living world and the intuition of an underlying, ineffable oneness pervading all things.

All three experiences of unity—through nature, international travel, and contemplative spirituality—came together and integrated with the sense of responsibility Steven learned from his grandfather. It was what motivated him in the 1990s to join the Earth Charter initiative, which involved a decade-long, worldwide dialogue on creating an ethical framework for building a just, sustainable, and peaceful global society, and to accept the invitation of the Earth Charter Commission, led by Maurice Strong and Mikhail Gorbachev, to chair the Earth Charter International Drafting Committee. Steven, working with the Drafting Committee and Commission supported by the Earth Charter Secretariat, managed to distill the common values and shared goals in the disparate visions of the hundreds of organizations and thousands of individuals who participated in the consultation and drafting process. The Earth Charter was launched in 2000 and has been endorsed by more than seven thousand organizations worldwide, including UNESCO, the International Union for Conservation of Nature, and many governments. Ecological integrity and sustainable development are central themes in the charter, and these goals are viewed as inseparable from the eradication of poverty, equitable economic development, respect for human rights, democracy, and peace.

While he was working on the Earth Charter, Steven was also teaching at Middlebury College. Among his courses were some that dealt with environmental ethics and the state of the world. Students could become discouraged and depressed by what they were learning about climate change, the loss of biodiversity, economic inequality, and other negative trends.

Drawing on what he had seen and learned from his Earth Charter work, he'd tell them: "You have a choice. All over the world in every culture there are visionary women and men doing beautiful work in the effort to build a better world, and they are making a real difference. You can sit here feeling helpless, overwhelmed by the bad news. Or you can go out and join these courageous people."

He would remind them that we don't know how the future will unfold. Improbable things happen: The Soviet Union collapsed without a shot being fired. Apartheid in South Africa was ended without a bloody revolution.

"No one predicted these turns of events," Steven says. "Terrible things can happen and definitely will if we give in to despair and apathy. However, if we join the extraordinary women and men leading creative movements for positive change, there is every reason for hope."

OUR INDIVIDUAL HEALTH and flourishing depend on our choice to awaken. So do the health and flourishing of our schools, workplaces, governments—and the planet. When we engage in our relationships, jobs, communities, and the environment with an awakened heart, we act in relation to a larger reality. If transcendent practice is the on-ramp to awakened awareness, a moral code is the off-ramp, the place where we take our spiritual perceptual capacities and merge them into our lives of service and contribution, making choices and decisions that reflect that we are guided and loved, that we belong to one another, that we're all related in the family of life.

Twenty years ago, Dr. Kenneth Kendler's twin study lit the path for my early investigation into the awakened brain. It was a remarkable study for its time, as it showed that our human capacity for spirituality is innate. Twin studies give us a broad picture of our genetic structure. They can tell us that as we develop, this proportion of our identity is socialized, and this proportion is innate—from our genes. When we add to this structural research on genotyping we start to identify *single genes* within the genetic proportion that contribute to who we are and become. Further research will begin to illuminate the epigenetic effect—how the genes synergize and work together as a symphony. For now, genetic research is helping identify particular instruments in that symphony.

Our collaborative Columbia team began to look at possible genetic correlates of depression and spirituality. We identified four single candidate genes associated with the neurotransmitters in the brain systems of depression and spirituality, and assessed these genes in the children and grandchildren of individuals at high and low risk for depression. We found that dopamine, serotonin, one of their transporters (called VMAT1), and oxytocin are all positively associated with a high level of importance of spirituality or religion. The genes for the neurotransmitters associated with bonding, transcendence, vitality in life, and a deep sense of peace and well-being are *within the system of the awakened brain,* and all directly correlate with personal spirituality. Interestingly, these same genes are correlated with both personal spirituality *and* depression, but in opposite dominant-recessive directions, suggesting once again that depression and spiritual awareness share some common physiology—that there is shared neural ground between spirituality on the one hand and depression on the other.

We all have the neural wiring for awakened awareness. What do recessive and dominant genes suggest? Only that just as some people see color more vividly, with more rods and cones in their eyes, so some people see the hues of awakened awareness more readily. Let this not be another realm for ranking or comparing ourselves to others. We all have what we need for awakened awareness, a doorway into a broad range of personal journeys and adventures, a common portal to a more unified and loving world. We share a foundational, neural, genetic common ground, *and* we each uniquely experience awakened life based on our own vibrant perceptual constellation.

Our work on single candidate genes brings high resolution to Dr. Kendler's landmark twin study on the general heritable component of spirituality. He found that one-third of the impact on our spirituality comes from genes. That means that two-thirds of the impact on our spirituality comes from how we cultivate our natural capacity. Spiritual awakening depends more on *the deliberate use of our inner life* than it does on our relative endowment from biology. Biology is a contributing factor to our capacity—but it doesn't stand alone to define our destiny. Each one of us has a choice in how we engage with the world. This can give us enormous respect and compassion for ourselves and for every person, because we all exist within the shared landscape of spirituality. **We are all on a path of awakening, again and again facing new challenges, closing and opening doors, moving ever and always toward greater awakening.**

We have the capacity for effective, creative, connected, and fulfilling lives. And together, we have the capacity to build an awakened society where schools embrace the responsibility and opportunity to nurture the spiritual core of all children. Where going to work doesn't just mean serving a function and getting a paycheck, but supplies us with the opportunity to further our own calling and contribution, and nurture our care for others. Where leaders get up and walk around and ask those they serve, "What's going on in your world? How's your soul today?" Where justice is practiced through the lens of interconnectedness and love. Where seemingly irreconciled people can open common ground. Where we treat all other living beings and systems as part of an encompassing, interconnected web of life. Where all areas of our lives and culture invite us to use our awakened brains to become aware of the bigger reality that we otherwise miss, and to translate that information and inspiration into decisions and actions that serve the highest good.

CONCLUSION

ISAIAH AND THE GEESE

One April afternoon Isaiah, Leah, and Lila were just home from school, sitting at the kitchen table drawing with markers and eating snacks. Isaiah, blond, robust, and hearty, was coloring people with heads a bright sunshine yellow. Lila, her chin-length brown hair worn with bangs, in her customary dress and action shorts. Leah, artistic, gentle, and focused, half smiling as she drew our family; Isaiah appearing on the page like her fraternal twin; Lila like a much smaller version of herself, freckles dotting her face. Suddenly, Isaiah looked out the window and cried, "Oh, no!"

I looked out where he pointed, at the river still brimming with whitecap waves from the late thaw. A group of young geese was fighting the waves, trying to cross the river. They seemed to be having trouble navigating the rough water. Isaiah rushed to the back door, barely pausing to pull on his boots before he ran outside, calling, "C'm'ere, geesie! C'm'ere, geesie!" He went right up to the water's edge, waving his arms at them, calling for their attention.

He stood on the slippery riverbank, at the edge of the water where I'd been swimming with all three of my children since they were babies, all of us lined up like ducks. Where we'd told Isaiah the story of how he'd come to us. "Mommy prayed for Isaiah," we'd say. "Daddy prayed for Isaiah. Pop-pop prayed for Isaiah. Grandma prayed for Isaiah. And then we took a train to an airplane to a car, and we ran up a hill, and there was Isaiah." We'd throw him in the air. "We found Isaiah!" we'd call. "We found Isaiah!" He'd shriek with delight. As he got a bit older, we would point upstream to the gentle waves, saying, "Isaiah, you came down this river, you are our baby Moses." He'd talk to the frogs and the ducks, drag his toes through the mud on the shore, sing-say, "I'm your baby Moses, yes, I'm your baby Moses." He never doubted that he was loved, that he belonged to the river, to us.

Until one recent day, when I drove him and his fellow eight-year-old best friend home from soccer practice. They were whispering in the back seat. "Mama, Mama," Isaiah suddenly said. "Jake says I'm not Jewish, my name's not Miller, and you're not my mother."

A lump rose in my throat. "But Isaiah," I said, "don't you remember?"

"Oh!" he exclaimed, and turned back to Jake. "I'm baby Moses," he said.

They bent their heads together, whispering fiercely.

"Mama?" Isaiah said again. This time there was real anxiety in his voice. "Mama, what about the woman who gave me up?"

I took a breath, summoning the words to tell him about the letters we'd been told she left at the hospital after his birth, praying I'd find the right way to explain her decision. It felt like the longest breath I ever took. I exhaled, prolonging the moment when I'd have to open my mouth and speak. But before I could say anything, Isaiah said, "Oh, I know. God whispered in her ear and said that you were crying for me."

In a breath, he went from an achieving awareness sense of fracture and abandonment to an awakened awareness that he is loved, that the world is full of love.

I watched him now on the riverbank, half afraid he'd lose his footing, ready to run outside in a flash and pull him in. He was still calling to the little geese. And suddenly something remarkable happened. They began to swim toward him. He called with an encouraging tone, "Come here, geesie," and waved his arms. They weren't afraid of him. He began to walk down the bank, and they followed along in the water as he led them to a shallow, steady place in the river where they could safely cross. He waited there until each one had made it to the other shore. When he turned toward the house to come inside, a huge smile lit his face.

He'd seen the geese with awakened attention, connection, and heart. While the kids had been coloring at the table, I had been fixated on my computer screen, my attention focused in one top-down direction. Isaiah had noticed the struggling geese that had been completely invisible to me. And while I was working furiously, pressed for time, trying to get as much as I could done before the kids needed to switch gears, Isaiah had not only noticed the geese but also known them and their predicament in relation to himself. He perceived them not as completely separate entities, but as beings whose experience had something to do with him.

Each one of us is born with this innate endowment of awareness. If this awakened awareness is supported as we grow up, we stay in dialogue with life. We benefit from creative guidance, love, and the embrace of life. Chronic dysthymia, the common suffering of disconnection, is less likely for the naturally awakened child who stays awakened. Watching my son brought my epidemiology work from twenty years before powerfully to mind. When we awaken, we are 80 percent less likely to face an episode of depression. This is our own and our children's path to an inspired life: to sustain and validate our innate way of being.

When we're living with an awakened brain, with achieving and awakened modes in balance, we are using the fullness of who we are and how we're wired to perceive. Our awakened brain is foundational to human knowledge and history; the call for awakened awareness reverberates across our diverse religious, cultural, and ethical traditions, and through global art and music, and humanitarian service and altruism. The awakened brain is our seat of perception for the transcendent and immanent. It's our internal point-wave function that alerts us to a felt guiding presence and the sacredness in daily life. It can be fostered by a broad span of actions, reflections, and practices; expressed across a range of symbols and languages. When we bring this fuller awareness and knowledge to our families, communities, schools, and governments, we create a more ethical and sustainable world—and we receive more meaning and purpose from our lives. We effect far more for ourselves, other people, and our fellow living beings.

This is what my quest for my family and my quest for a new science of spirituality have taught me: that each and every moment we have a choice of how we see ourselves and the world. We can live chasing goals and rewards, lost in worries and regrets. Or we can awaken to the true fabric of the world, an evolving tapestry that we both behold and help create, in which every thread matters and no strand stands alone. We can live in isolation, or we can awaken to the common knowing and communication among all living beings, and to a deep, felt alignment with the source of consciousness.

When Isaiah came inside the house, his cheeks were red from

the cold. He grinned at me. "Did you see that, Mom?" he said. "I helped them and they followed me." He gave me a quick happy hug before he raced back to join his sisters at the table. I heard them giggle together, and saw them gaze out the window at the little geese bobbing along in the grass on the opposite shore, digging energetically for food.

I thought of the residents on Unit 6, where my quest began, and all the people I'd met in the twenty-plus years since our makeshift service in the back kitchen. From Iliana to Gary Weaver, anxious adolescents to grieving parents, marginalized youth to leaders of social change, and all who'd experienced the healing that comes when we see the world that we're wired to see. The awakened brain, and the reality it illuminates, is not the privileged insight of a lucky few—but the birthright of all.

ACKNOWLEDGMENTS

This book was created by a team. The great Mark Warren and Chayenne Skeete and your exceptional colleagues at Random House, my deepest gratitude to you for bringing the truths revealed in this science into the center of our society. Now, at this time of tremendous need, your bold leadership and direction allow us to join together with readers in a transformative moment. You are the culture-makers of our time.

From its formation, this book has been an energetic, creative collaboration. I had the best co-creators in the world in the highly awakened team at Idea Architects. The IA vision, values, and artistic acumen allow us to share the pathway of science, as science actually is developed, and to tell that journey alongside my inner quest and those of fellow researchers, activists, and civic and business leaders.

Doug Abrams, you serve the highest cause with your rare genius and generous heart. You bring your innovative eye and the very finest values to every moment: from a creative whiteboard session; to auction; to leading your exceptionally well-hired, cultivated, and genuinely loved IA team; and even to our narrative exploration walking through the California Redwoods. Together with the wonderfully gifted Lara Love Hardin, you turn the ideas and discoveries trapped inside academia into culture-changing opportunities.

Esmé Schwall Weigand, my co-writer, you are an artist in the deepest sense. Your prose works at multiple levels of epistemology; your turns of phrase hit head and heart. I am profoundly grateful for your love of this science, for the respect and tenderness with which you wrote my story and those of other contributors, and for your all-in valuing of the larger vision. You are the writer's equivalent of a Stanislavski in your complete and total immersion: twice visiting my home, splashing in the Saugatuck, sitting in on Columbia lectures, sharing dinner with my children and parents, and even taking a drive over to the "Lost Plaza."

Rachel Neumann, you could edit a tanker into a cigarette boat. So brilliantly you see the spine inside the hearty body of the drafts. Your sophisticated knowledge of the publishing field allows us to speak squarely into the culture. Ty Love, you are so highly capable, always aware of the mission and working right on the cusp of cultural transformation. Eric Rayman, you are a keen-eyed, elegant publishing lawyer.

My collaborations with my graduate students over twenty years stream throughout this scientific journey. My current and former students, our collaboration shines throughout the reference pages. Many of you are shown by name on listed articles as co-authors of important research, drawn from well over a hundred articles and chapters that we have developed together as a lab. Every single one of you has been a vital co-author, co-thinker, co-statistician, co-writer, and co-journeyer. Thank you for your love of truth, and for your keen eyes and professional courage as together we quested into this new scientific terrain.

My mentors, with sharp, clear eyes, and equally warm hearts, you resolutely encouraged my inquiry well before it found a place in the center of our field and society. My tremendous gratitude to you: Martin Seligman, Myrna Weissman, Carol Dweck, Mahzarin Banaji, David Shaffer, Tom James, Steven Rockefeller, Frank Peabody, and the late Susan Nolen-Hoeksema. My heartfelt gratitude to the Weissman team at Columbia University Medical School for twenty years of collaboration: Myrna, Priya, Connie, Marc, Steven, Adi, Phil, Jurgen, James, Karl, and our beloved late Craig and Virginia. To the Yale team, for an outstanding four-year collaboration: Marc, Rajita, Iris, and Patrick.

Awakened awareness illuminates a path to inspired leadership, as revealed through the personal stories of some of our great national leaders: Steven Rockefeller, Tim Shriver, Bob Chapman, Tom Solhjem, Walter Fluker, and Mary Evelyn Tucker. Your force of outer impact forwards our society. Thank you for so generously sharing the quest that has led to inner awareness and your pathway to creating lifesaving work, for holding up your bright torch and in turn illuminating our journey.

My dearest depth of gratitude and appreciation to the eternally loving couple Colleen Weaver and the late Gary Weaver: You lifted up so many lives, certainly including my own. You love us all, whether merited or unmerited—as you would say, purely for being "G-d's precious children."

To our readers, we wrote this book for you. We are drawn together as part of a wave of change. Thank you for your awakened service to one another, for your openness to learning and growth, and for your loving care and support for all living beings of the planet.

My children, my loves: Leah, Lila, and Isaiah. You kick open the door to our inspired family life, all the time. Your daily awakened awareness is transcendent and immanent. Our family lives in a world infinitely larger because of you, bubbling with love, joy, and the flux of vitality and creativity. You use your awakened awareness to give.

Mom, Dad, and Mark—we had a superb start and now share an equally wonderful full run. You are a true blessing.

Philip, I could not have made the trip without you.

NOTES

INTRODUCTION

4   **In 2017, 66.6 million Americans** Substance Abuse and Mental Health Services Administration (2018). Key substance use and mental health indicators in the United States: Results from the 2017 National Survey on Drug Use and Health (HHS Publication No. SMA 18-5068, NSDUH Series H-53). Rockville, MD: Center for Behavioral Health Statistics and Quality, Substance Abuse and Mental Health Services Administration. Retrieved from https://www .samhsa.gov/data/.

4   **Thirty-one percent of American adults** Harvard Medical School, 2007. National Comorbidity Survey (NCS) (2017, August 21). Retrieved from https://www.hcp.med.harvard.edu/ncs/index _php. Data Table 2: 12-month prevalence DSM-IV/WMH-CIDI disorders by sex and cohort. Harvard Medical School, 2007. National Comorbidity Survey (NCS) (2017, August 21). Retrieved from https://www.hcp.med.harvard.edu/ncs/index_php. Data Table 1: Lifetime prevalence DSM-IV/WMH-CIDI disorders by sex and cohort. Kessler R.C., Chiu W.T., Demier O. Merikangas K.R., Walters E.E. Prevalence, severity, and comorbidity of 12-month DSM-IV disorders in the National Comorbidity Survey Replication. *Arch Gen Psychiatry*. 2005 Jun; 62(6): 617–27. PMID: 15939839.

4   **264 million people** "Depression," World Health Organization, January 30, 2020, https://www.who.int/news-room/fact-sheets/detail/depression.

4   **third most costly disability** GBD 2017 Disease and Injury Incidence and Prevalence Collaborators (2018). Global, regional, and national incidence, prevalence, and years lived with disability for 354 diseases and injuries for 195 countries and territories, 1990–2017: A systematic analysis for the Global Burden of Disease Study 2017. *The Lancet*. Retrieved from https://www.who.int/news-room/fact-sheets/detail/depression. Wang, et al. (2007). Use of mental health services for anxiety, mood, and substance disorders in 17 countries in the WHO world mental health surveys. *The Lancet* 370(9590): 841–50. Retrieved from https://www.who.int/news-room/fact-sheets/detail/depression.

4   **Over 16 percent of youth** "Major Depression," National Institute of Mental Health, February 2019. Retrieved from https://www.nimh.nih.gov/health/statistics/major-depression.shtml.

4   *second leading cause of death* "Underlying Cause of Death, 1999–2019," CDC Wonder, Centers for Disease Control and Prevention, https://wonder.cdc.gov/controller/saved/D76/D91F023.

4   **A study of more than 67,000 college students** Liu, C.H., Stevens, C., Wong, S.H., et al. (2019). The prevalence and predictors of mental health diagnoses and suicide among U.S. college students: Implications for addressing disparities in service use. *Depression and Anxiety* 36(1): 8–17.

5   **Only *half* of treated patients** Ionescu, D.F., Rosenbaum, J.F., and Alpert, J.E. (2015). Pharmacological approaches to the challenge of treatment-resistant depression. *Dialogues in Clinical Neuroscience* 17(2): 111–26; Kato, M., Hori, H., Inoue, T., et al. (2020). Discontinuation of antidepressants after remission with antidepressant medication in major depressive disorder: A systematic review and meta-analysis. *Molecular Psychiatry*, https://doi.org/10.1038/s41380-020-0843-0. Culpepper, L., Muskin, P., and Stahl, S. (2015). Major depressive disorder: Understanding the significance of residual symptoms and balancing efficacy with tolerability. *American Journal of Medicine* 128(9A): S1–S15.

7   **The high-spiritual brain was healthier** Miller, L., Bansal, R., Wickramaratne, P., et al. (2014). Neuroanatomical correlates of religiosity and spirituality: A study in adults at high and low familial risk for depression. *JAMA Psychiatry* 71(2): 128–35.

CHAPTER 2: THE EMPTY KITCHEN

33   **For Sol and Rebecca** Miller, L. (1997). "Yom Kippur on a Psychiatric In-Patient Unit. Case reports of spiritual issues and interventions in psychotherapy." In Richards, P.S., and Bergin, A.E. (1997). *A Spiritual Strategy for Counseling and Psychotherapy,* APA Press, 275–80.

CHAPTER 3: STARS IN A DARK SKY

51   **I discovered something striking** Miller, L., Warner, V., Wickramaratne, P., and Weissman, M. (1997). Religiosity and depression: Ten-year follow-up of depressed mothers and offspring. *Journal of the American Academy of Child and Adolescent Psychiatry* 36(10): 1416–25.

CHAPTER 4: TWO SIDES OF THE SAME COIN

54   **Dr. Kenneth Kendler** Kendler, K.S., Gardner, C.O., and Prescott, C.A. (1997). Religion, psychopathology, and substance use and abuse: A multimeasure, genetic-epidemiologic study. *American Journal of Psychiatry* 154(3): 322–29.

61   **in the nationally representative sample of teens** Miller, L., Davies, M., and Greenwald, S. (2000). Religiosity and substance use and abuse among adolescents in the national comorbidity survey. *Journal of the American Academy of Child and Adolescent Psychiatry* 39(9): 1190–97.

CHAPTER 5: SOMEONE WATCHING OVER ME

78   **So in 1999, two years** Kendler, K.S., Gardner, C.O., and Prescott, C.A. (1999). Clarifying the relationship between religiosity and psychiatric illness: The impact of covariates and the specificity of buffering effects. *Twin Research* 2:137–44. Piedmont, R. (1999). Strategies for using the five-factor model of personality in religious research. *Journal of Psychology and Theology* 27(4): 338–50.

CHAPTER 7: WHEN INNER AND OUTER ALIGN

94   **One student—Lydia Cho** Cho, L., Miller, L.J., Hrastar, M.G., and Sutton, N. (2009). Synchronicity awareness intervention: An open trial. *Teachers College Record* 111(12): 2786–99.

95   **Dr. Marc Berman and his colleagues** Berman, M.G., Jonides, J., and Kapland, S. (2008). The cognitive benefits of interacting with nature. *Psychological Science* 19(12): 1207–12.

CHAPTER 9: THE CASTLE AND THE WAVE

118 **In trying to understand** Nolen-Hoeksema, S., Wisco, B.E., and Lyubomirsky, S. (2008). Rethinking rumination. *Association for Psychological Science* 3(5): 400–424. Lyobomirsky, S., Layous, K., Chancellor, J., and Nelson, S.K. (2015). Thinking about rumination: The scholarly contributions and intellectual legacy of Susan Nolen-Hoeksema. *Annual Review of Clinical Psychology* 11: 1–22.

120 **In 2004, the American** Miller, L. (2005). *Spiritual Awareness Psychotherapy.* DVD. American Psychological Association Psychotherapy Video Series.

126 **Some of the lead creators** Freedman, R., Lewis, D.A., Michels, R., et al. (2013). The initial field trials of DSM-5: New blooms and old thorns. *American Journal of Psychiatry* 170(1): 1–5.

127 **About one in ten** Pratt, L.A., Brody, D.J., and Gu, Q. (2011). Antidepressant use in persons aged 12 and over: United States, 2005–2008. National Center for Health Statistics Data Brief, No. 76.

127 **The high medication rates** Takayanagi, Y., Spira, A.P., Bienvenu, O.J., et al. (2015). Antidepressant use and lifetime history of mental disorders in a community sample: Results from the Baltimore epidemiologic catchment area study. *Journal of Clinical Psychiatry* 76(1): 40–44. Mark, T.L., Levit, K.R., Buck, J.A. (2009). Data points: Psychotropic drug prescriptions by medical specialty. *Psychiatric Services.* 60(9): https://doi.org/10.1176/ps.2009.60.9.1167.

127 **Antidepressants taken during pregnancy** Boukhris, T., Sheehy, O., Mottron, L., and Bérard, A. (2016). Antidepressant use during pregnancy and the risk of autism spectrum disorder in children. *JAMA Pediatrics* 170(2): 117–24. https://doi.org/10.1001/jamapediatrics .2015.3356. PMID: 26660917. Lugo-Candelas, C., Cha, J., Hong, S., et al. (2018). Associations between brain structure and connectivity in infants and exposure to Selective Serotonin Reuptake Inhibitors during pregnancy. *JAMA Pediatrics* 172(6): 525–33.

127 **And young adults taking high-dose** Sharma, T., Guski, L.S., Freund, N., and Gøtzsche, P.C. (2016). Suicidality and aggression during antidepressant treatment: Systematic review and meta-analyses based on clinical study reports. *BMJ* 352: i65. Fornaro, M., Anastasia, A., Valchera, A., et al. (2019). The FDA "black box" warning on antidepressant suicide risk in young adults: More harm than benefits? *Frontiers in Psychiatry.* https://doi.org/10.3389/fpsyt .2019.00294.

CHAPTER 10: A DIFFERENT LIFE

139 **A few years later** Barkin, S.H., Miller, L., and Luthar, S.S. (2015). Filling the void: Spiritual development among adolescents of the affluent. *Journal of Religion and Health* 54(3): 844–61. https://doi .org/10.1007/s10943-015-0048-z. Luthar, S. (2003). The culture of affluence: Psychological costs of material wealth. *Child Development* 74(6): 1581–93. Rabin, Roni Caryn. Study Links Depression to Thinning of Brain's Cortex, *New York Times,* March 24, 2009.

141 **I developed a long-term** Miller, L., Wickramaratne, P., Gameroff, M.J., et al. (2012). Religiosity and major depression in adults at high risk: A ten-year prospective study. *American Journal of Psychiatry* 169(1): 89–94. https://doi.org/10.1176/appi.ajp.2011.10121823.

CHAPTER 11: WIRED FOR SPIRITUALITY

147 **In 2009, researchers** Peterson, B.S., and Weissman, M.M. (2011). A brain-based endophenotype for major depressive disorder. *Annual Review of Medicine* 62: 461–74. https://doi.org/10.1146/annurev -med-010510-095632. Dubin, M.J., Weissman, M.M., Xu, D., et al. (2012). Identification of a circuit-based endophenotype for familial depression. *Psychiatry Research: Neuroimaging* 201(3): 175–81. https:// doi.org/10.1016/j.pscychresns.2011.11.007. Rabin, Roni Caryn. Study Links Depression to Thinning of Brain's Cortex, *New York Times,* March 24, 2009.

150 **The subjects for whom spirituality** Miller, L., Bansal, R., Wickramaratne, P., et al. (2014). Neuroanatomical correlates of religiosity and spirituality: A study in adults at high and low familial risk for depression. *JAMA Psychiatry* 71(2): 128–35.

152 **We had study participants** Tenke, C.E., Kayser, J., Miller, L., et al. (2013). Neuronal generators of posterior EEG alpha reflect individual differences in prioritizing personal spirituality. *Biological Psychology* 94: 426–32. Tenke, C.E., Kayser, J., Svob, C., et al. (2017). Association of posterior EEG alpha with prioritization of religion or spirituality: A replication and extension at 20-year follow-up. *Biological Psychology* 124: 79–86.

CHAPTER 12: THE TWO MODES OF AWARENESS

156 **We worked together** Miller, L., Balodis, I.M., McClintock, C.H., et al. (2018). Neural correlates of personalized spiritual experiences. *Cerebral Cortex* 29(6): 2331–38.

156 **Given that late adolescence** Miller, L. (2013). Spiritual awakening and depression in adolescents: A unified pathway or "two sides of the same coin." *Bulletin of the Menninger Clinic* 77(4): 332–48. Barton, Y.A., Barkin, S.H., and Miller, L. (2017). Deconstructing depression: A latent profile analysis of potential depressive subtypes in emerging adults. *Spirituality in Clinical Practice* 4(1): 1–21.

161 **Overall, our study** McClintock, C.H., et al. (2019). Spiritual experiences are related to engagement of a ventral frontotemporal functional brain network: Implications for prevention and treatment of behavioral and substance addictions. *Journal of Behavioral Addictions* 8(4): 678–91.

CHAPTER 13: INTEGRATION IS KEY

170 **When we measured DTI** Xu, J., McClintock, C.H., Balodis, I.M., Miller, L., and Potenza, M.N. (2018). Openness to changing religious views is related to radial diffusivity in the genu of the corpus callosum in an initial study of healthy young adults. *Frontiers in Psychology* 9(330): 1–8.

171 **Interestingly, some of the same** Bora, E., Harrison, B.J., Davey, C.G., et al. (2012). Meta-analysis of volumetric abnormalities in cortico-striatal-pallidal-thalamic circuits in major depressive disorder. *Psychological Medicine* 42: 671–81. Chen, G., Hu, X., Li, L., et al. (2016). Disorganization of white matter architecture in major depressive disorder: A meta-analysis of diffusion tensor imaging with tract-based spatial statistics. *Scientific Reports* 6(21825). Choi, K.S., Holtzheimer, P.E., Franco, A.R., et al. (2014). Reconciling variable findings of white matter integrity in major depressive disorder. *Neuropsychopharmacology* 39: 1332–39. Jiang, X., Shen, Y., Yao, J., et al. (2019). Connectome analysis of functional and structural hemispheric brain networks in major depressive disorder. *Translational Psychiatry* 9: 136. Liao, Y., Huang, X., Wu, Q., et al. (2013). Is depression a disconnection syndrome? Meta-analysis of diffusion tensor imaging studies in patients with MDD. *Journal of Psychiatry and Neuroscience* 38: 49–56. Peters, S.K., Dunlop, K., and Downar, J. (2016). Cortico-striatal-thalamic loop circuits of the salience network: A central pathway in psychiatric disease and treatment. *Frontiers in Systems Neuroscience* 10: 104. Schilbach, L., Müller, V.I., Hoffstaedter, F., et al. (2014). Meta-analytically informed network analysis of resting state fMRI reveals hyperconnectivity in an introspective socio-affective network in depression. *PLOS ONE*. https://doi.org/10.1371/journal.pone.0094973. Cisler, J.M., James,

G.A., Tripathi, S., et al. (2012). Differential functional connectivity within an emotion regulation neural network among individuals resilient and susceptible to the depressogenic effects of early life stress. *Psychological Medicine* 43(3): 507–18. Lu, Q., Li, H., Luo, G., et al. (2013). Impaired prefrontal-amygdala effective connectivity is responsible for the dysfunction of emotion processing in major depressive disorder: A dynamic causal modeling study on MEG. *Neuroscience Letters* 523(2): 125–30. McCabe, C., and Mishor, Z. (2011). Antidepressant medications reduce subcortical-cortical resting-state functional connectivity in healthy volunteers. *Neuroimage* 57(4): 1317–23.

172 **But those who were high in openness** Antinori, A., Carter, O.L., and Smillie, L.D. (2017). Seeing it both ways: Openness to experience and binocular rivalry suppression. *Journal of Research in Personality* 68: 15–22.

173 **awaken, transform, and expand even through trauma** Tsai, J., et al. (2014). Post-traumatic growth among veterans in the USA: Results from the National Health and Resilience in Veterans Study. *Psychological Medicine* 45: 165–79.

CHAPTER 14: AWAKENED ATTENTION

176 **a large body of scientific research** Zeidan, F., Baumgartner, J.N., and Coghill, R.C. (2019). The neural mechanisms of mindfulness-based pain relief: A functional magnetic resonance imaging-based review and primer. *Pain Reports* 4(4), doi: 10.1097/ PR9.0000000000000759. Zeidan, F., Martucci, K.T., Kraft, R.A., et al. (2014). Neural correlates of mindfulness meditation-related anxiety relief. *Social Cognitive and Affective Neuroscience* 9(6): 751–59. https://doi.org/10.1093/scan/nst041. Brambilla, C.A., and Serretti, A. (2010). Functional neural correlates of mindfulness meditation in comparison with psychotherapy, pharmacotherapy and placebo effect: Is there a link? *Acta Neuropsychiatrica* 22: 104–17. Creswell, J.D., Way, B., Eisenberger, N.I., and Leiberman, M.D. (2007). Neural correlates of dispositional mindfulness during affect labeling. *Psychosomatic Medicine* 69: 560–65.

176 **In one study, people** Janes, A.C., Datko, M., Roy, A., et al. (2019). Quitting starts in the brain: A randomized controlled trial of app-based mindfulness shows decreases in neural responses to smoking cues that predict reductions in smoking. *Neuropsychopharmacology* 44: 1631–38. Kober, H., Brewer, J.A., Height, K.L., and Sinha, R. (2017). Neural stress reactivity relates to smoking outcomes and dif-

ferentiates between mindfulness and cognitive-behavioral treatments. *NeuroImage* 151: 4–13.

177 **Gregory Bratman, an ecologist** Bratman, G.N., Hamilton, J.P., Hahn, K.S., et al. (2015). Nature experience reduces rumination and subgenual prefrontal cortex activation. *Proceedings of the National Academy of Sciences* 112(28): 8567–72. Bratman, G.N., Daily, G.C., Levy, B.J., and Gross, J.J. (2015). The benefits of nature experience: Improved affect and cognition. *Landscape and Urban Planning* 138: 41–50.

177 **Mindfulness and exposure to nature** McClintock, C.H., et al. (2019). How spirituality may mitigate against stress and related mental disorders: A review and preliminary neurobiological evidence. *Current Behavioral Neuroscience Reports* 6: 253–62.

CHAPTER 15: AWAKENED CONNECTION

197 **Beginning in 1987** Grinberg-Zylberbaum, J. (1982). The orbitals of consciousness: a neurosyntergic approach to the discrete levels of conscious experience. Central Intelligence Agency. https://www .cia.gov/library/readingroom/docs/CIA-RDP96-00792R0007001 30001-6.pdf. Grinberg-Zylberbaum, J. (1981). The transformation of neuronal activity into conscious experience: The syntergic theory. *Journal of Social and Biological Structures* 4(3): 201–10.

198 **Andrew Newberg, a neuroscientist** Newberg, A. (2018). *Neurotheology: How Science Can Enlighten Us About Spirituality* (Chapter 11). New York: Columbia University Press. Newberg, A. (2016). *Principles of Neurotheology.* New York: Routledge (Taylor & Francis).

198 **Numerous EEG studies** Fabbri-Destro, M., and Rizzolatti, G. (2008). Mirror neurons and mirror systems in monkeys and humans. *Physiology* (American Physiology Society) 23(3): 171–79. https://doi .org/10.1152/physiol.00004.2008. Rizzolatti, G., Fabbri-Destro, M., and Cattaneo, L. (2009). Mirror neurons and their clinical relevance. *Nature Clinical Practice* 5(10): 24–34.

199 **A fascinating study** Goldstein, P., Weissman-Fogel, I., Dumas, G., and Shamay-Tsoory, S.G. (2018). Brain-to-brain coupling during handholding is associated with pain reduction. *Proceedings of the National Academy of Sciences of the United States of America* 115(11).

201 **Dr. Jeanne Achterberg showed** Schwartz, S., and Dossey, L. (2012). "Nonlocality, Intention, and Observer Effects in Healing Studies: Laying a Foundation for the Future." In Miller, L. (ed.), *Oxford University Press Handbook* (Chapter 34). New York: Oxford

University Press. Achterberg, J. (2002). *Imagery in Healing: Shamanism and Modern Medicine*. Boulder, CO: Shambhala Publications.

204 **engaging this awareness** Mastropieri, B., Schussel, L., Forbes, D., and Miller, L. (2015). Inner resources for survival: Integrating interpersonal psychotherapy with spiritual visualization with homeless youth. *Journal of Religion and Health* 54(3): 903–21. Schussel, L., and Miller, L. (2013). Best self visualization method with high-risk youth. *Journal of Clinical Psychology* 69(8): 1–10.

CHAPTER 16: AWAKENED HEART

220 **five common spiritual phenotypes** McClintock, C.H., Lau, E., and Miller, L. (2016). Phenotypic dimensions of spirituality: Implications for mental health in China, India, and the United States. *Frontiers in Psychology* 7(1600): 1–16. McClintock, C.H., et al. (2018). Multidimensional understanding of religiosity/spirituality: Relationship to major depression and familial risk. *Psychological Medicine* 1–10. https.//doi.org/10.1017/50033291718003276.

221 **Using survey questions** Miller, L., Wickramaratne, P., Hao, X., et al. Neuroanatomical protection of love and altruism against depression. Submitted.

230 **Ilias Kamitsis** Kamitsis, I., and Francis, J.P. (2013). Spirituality mediates the relationship between engagement with nature and psychological wellbeing. *Journal of Environmental Psychology* 36: 136–43.

230 **Science reveals** Swimme, B.T., and Tucker, M.E. (2011). *Journey of the Universe*. New Haven, CT: Yale University Press.

234 **Earth Charter initiative** Earth Charter website, https://earthcharter.org.

236 **Our collaborative Columbia team** Anderson, M.R., Miller, L., Wickramaratne, P., et al. (2017). Genetic correlates of spirituality/religion and depression: A study in offspring and grandchildren at high and low familial risk for depression. *Spirituality in Clinical Practice* 4(1): 43–63.

INDEX

ABOUT THE AUTHOR

Lisa Miller, PhD, is the *New York Times* bestselling author of *The Spiritual Child: The New Science on Parenting for Health and Lifelong Thriving* and a professor in the clinical psychology program at Teachers College, Columbia University. She is the founder and director of the Spirituality Mind Body Institute, the first Ivy League graduate program in spirituality and psychology, and for over a decade has held joint appointments in the department of psychiatry at Columbia University medical school. Her innovative research has been published in more than one hundred empirical, peer-reviewed articles in leading journals, including *Cerebral Cortex, The American Journal of Psychiatry,* and the *Journal of the American Academy of Child and Adolescent Psychiatry.* She lives in Connecticut with her husband and their three children.